# HALLOW GROUND

## CHURCHYARDS OF GLOUCESTERSHIRE AND THE COTSWOLDS

## HILARY LEES

*Hilary Lees*

**THORNHILL PRESS**
Publishers

**About the author:**
Hilary Lees has been writing regularly for a
number of years, and contributes to a number of
well-known magazines. She has lived in
Gloucestershire for thirty years and is married
with grown-up children. Hallowed Ground is her
first book.

First published in Great Britain by Thornhill Press Ltd
1993

ISBN 0 946328 38 2

Printed in Great Britain by Ian Allan Printing Ltd,
Coombelands House, Addlestone, Surrey KT15 1HY.

# Acknowledgements

I would like to thank all those people whose help
and interest have contributed to the writing of
this book, including the following:

Tom Chester
Dr Susan A Clarke
Eve Dennis and the Church and Conservation
    Project.
Dr David Glue
David Haigh
English Heritage
David Smith and the Gloucestershire Record
    Office
Jonathan MacKechnie-Jarvis, Diocesan Advisory
    Committee
Allen Meredith and English Nature
Colin Studholme, Gloucestershire Trust for
    Nature Conservation
Geoffrey N Wright
Rory Young

and especially, Joan Lake.

Excerpt from Betjeman's Churchyards
    reproduced by kind permission of John
    Murray.
Illustration (Roman tombstone) on page 12 by
    courtesy of the Corinium Museum,
    Cirencester.
Photographs, unless stated otherwise, by the
    author.
Cover photograph of Elmore churchyard
    by Derek Morgan.
Map, and line drawings from brass plates in
    Edgeworth Churchyard by Mary Penny.

*To Edmund, with love.*

# Contents

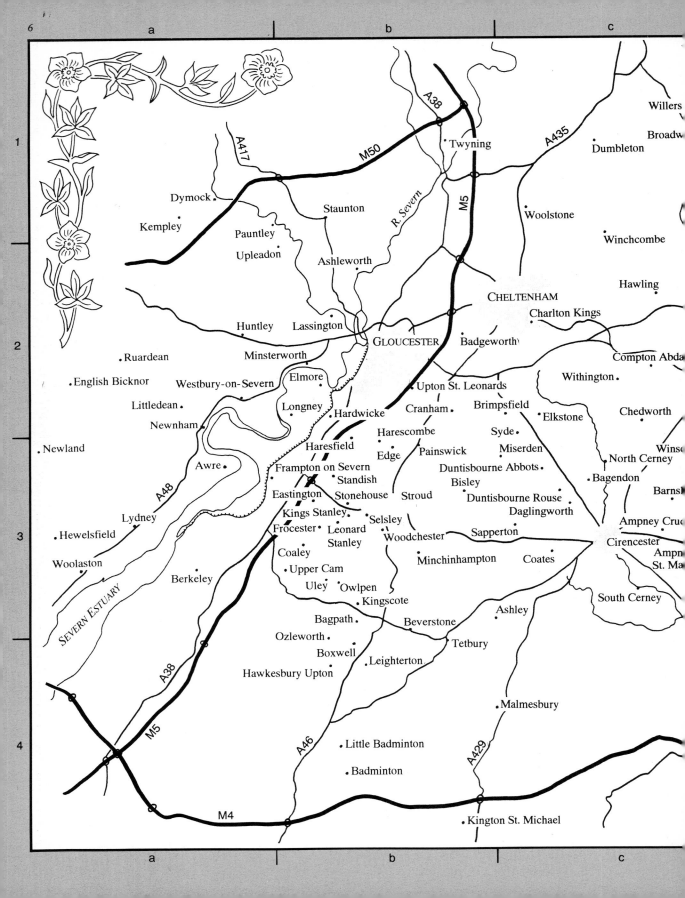

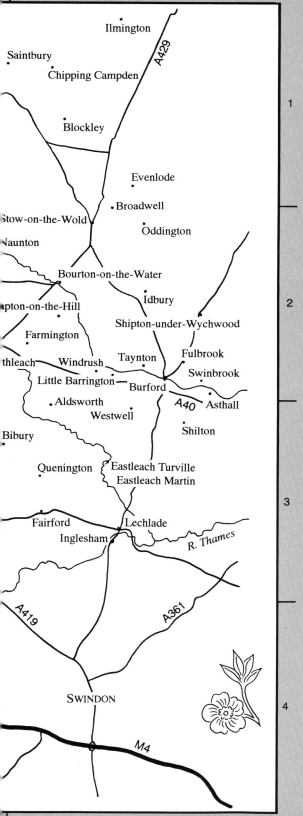

# WHERE TO FIND THE
## CHURCHYARDS
### OF
## GLOUCESTERSHIRE AND THE
## COTSWOLDS

| | | | |
|---|---|---|---|
| Aldsworth | d3 | Kempley | a1 |
| Ampney Crucis | c3 | Kings Stanley | b3 |
| Ampney St. Mary | c3 | Kingscote | b3 |
| Ashleworth | b2 | Kington St. Michael | b4 |
| Ashley | c3 | Lassington | b2 |
| Asthall | d2 | Lechlade | d3 |
| Awre | a3 | Leighterton | b4 |
| Badgeworth | b2 | Leonard Stanley | b3 |
| Badminton | b4 | Little Badminton | b4 |
| Bagendon | c3 | Little Barrington | d2 |
| Bagpath | b3 | Littledean | a2 |
| Barnsley | c3 | Longney | b2 |
| Berkeley | a3 | Lydney | a3 |
| Beverstone | b3 | Malmesbury | c4 |
| Bibury | c3 | Minchinhampton | b3 |
| Bisley | b3 | Minsterworth | b2 |
| Blockley | d1 | Miserden | c3 |
| Bourton-on-the-Water | d2 | Naunton | c2 |
| Boxwell | b4 | Newland | a3 |
| Brimpsfield | c2 | Newnham | a2 |
| Broadway | c1 | North Cerney | c3 |
| Broadwell | d2 | Northleach | c2 |
| Burford | d2 | Oddington | d2 |
| Charlton Kings | c2 | Owlpen | b3 |
| Chedworth | c2 | Ozleworth | b4 |
| Chipping Campden | d1 | Painswick | b3 |
| Cirencester | c3 | Pauntley | a1 |
| Clapton-on-the-Hill | d2 | Quenington | d3 |
| Coaley | b3 | Ruardean | a2 |
| Coates | c3 | Saintbury | c1 |
| Compton Abdale | c2 | Sapperton | c3 |
| Cranham | b2 | Selsley | b3 |
| Daglingworth | c3 | Shilton | d3 |
| Dumbleton | c1 | Shipton-under- | |
| Duntisbourne Abbots | c3 | -Wychwood | d2 |
| Duntisbourne Rouse | c3 | South Cerney | c3 |
| Dymock | a1 | Standish | b3 |
| Eastington | b3 | Staunton | b1 |
| Eastleach Martin | d3 | Stonehouse | b3 |
| Eastleach Turville | d3 | Stow-on-the-Wold | d2 |
| Edge | b3 | Stroud | b3 |
| Elkstone | c2 | Swinbrook | d2 |
| Elmore | b2 | Syde | c2 |
| English Bicknor | a2 | Taynton | d2 |
| Evenlode | d1 | Tetbury | b4 |
| Fairford | d3 | Twyning | b1 |
| Farmington | d2 | Uley | b3 |
| Frampton on Severn | a3 | Upleadon | b2 |
| Frocester | b3 | Upper Cam | b3 |
| Fulbrook | d2 | Upton St. Leonards | b2 |
| Hardwicke | b2 | Westbury-on-Severn | a2 |
| Harescombe | b3 | Westwell | d3 |
| Haresfield | b3 | Willersey | c1 |
| Hawkesbury Upton | b4 | Winchcombe | c1 |
| Hawling | c2 | Windrush | d2 |
| Hewelsfield | a3 | Winson | c3 |
| Huntley | a2 | Withington | c2 |
| Idbury | d2 | Woodchester | b3 |
| Ilmington | d1 | Woolaston | a3 |
| Inglesham | d3 | Woolstone | c1 |

# God's Acre

For most of us, the church is the centre of the village, probably the most ancient and most sacred site in the parish. The tall beckoning finger of a spire or the dumpy digit of a tower that says I am here, this is a place, a community, a collection of people connected by the fact that they live in this parish, this town or village. For hundreds of years the church and the God's Acre on which it stands has been the physical and spiritual centre of community life.

Yet how often do we walk up the path to the church door without looking to right or left? How many people have walked right round their own church, looking at the tombs and head-stones of the churchyard, running their thumbs over rounded cherub cheeks, stooping to read the legends of dead infants, loyal servants, public figures, all long forgotten?

To walk through an ancient churchyard is to step back in time; to feel that unique, evocative sensation that is a mixture of nostalgia, quietude and the vague reverence that we all have for death.

Each churchyard has a character of its own; some are quiet, untrodden, overgrown, a haven for wild flowers and birds, while the gravestones are eaten into by ivy, tilted towards the sky by invading roots and plants. Others may be tidied and mown until they are devoid of all character, or even cleared altogether, the stones removed to the boundary wall to make way for the all-consuming mower.

It is part of the nature of Gloucestershire and the Cotswolds that stone which has been hewn from the ground to build the houses, the churches, and walls gives a uniformity of texture and tone as though the buildings have grown out of the ground. In the same way the church and the churchyard are tied together physically: the churchyard is the setting for the church; it lends character and proportion, enables one to step back and see the building in the context of its surroundings. The churchyard may have been there hundreds of years longer than the church that now stands in it, but the feeling that this is a living place of worship, albeit among the dead, welds together the building and the sacred ground that surrounds it.

In this area we have an outstanding heritage in our churches. From the great wool churches of Northleach and Chipping Campden to the little Norman churches of Oddington or Ozleworth we have period architecture for which the Cotswolds is justly famous, as well as the priceless treasures of murals, frescoes, monuments and carvings that they contain.

In our churchyards are treasures of a different sort, many of them also some of the best in the country. Painswick has what is probably the finest collection anywhere of Georgian tombs; Standish has one of the oldest inscriptions, still legible after 350 years; and Elmore, a tiny hamlet on the banks of the Severn, has a deep-carved table tomb of astonishing intricacy and symbolism.

The inscriptions bring to life the craft of lettering of years ago and how it developed to modern times; antiquated spelling, letters joined together or run on to the next line when they ran out of space. Beautiful decorative lettering on brass plates almost as good as the day it was done; and epitaphs, moral, sentimental, or simply factual, recording the feelings of generations ago.

A church and the surrounding churchyard reflect the area it serves in terms of wealth, occupations and attitudes. To archaeologists and historians they are a mine of information; they tell the history of the ordinary people of a parish for nearly 400 years; of how they felt about life, death and human frailty; about what they did, and how and why they died; of muggings and drownings and dread disease. The churchyard may contain outcast items from the church; repairs and gravedigging may reveal coffins and grave covers from early dates; where this has happened they have sometimes been incorporated into the church building, like the grave covers in the north wall of Beverston church. Coins and pottery may be unearthed from commercial activities in the churchyard in mediaeval times.

Gloucestershire is a particularly fine example of changes in style from the simple rustic designs still predominating in the Forest of Dean to the imposing monuments erected in the Cotswolds to landed gentry and wealthy wool merchants.

Nearly every one of Gloucestershire's four hundred or so churchyards has something to offer; perhaps a breathtaking Cotswold view, or an ancient creaking yew tree, almost as old as life itself. Together they add up to hundreds of acres of unsprayed and unploughed grassland, and their value as nature conservation areas has only recently begun to be appreciated. Churchyards are open to all to enjoy, whether it's a carpet of daffodils in spring, or a tree ablaze with autumn colour. Or just an oasis of peace and tranquillity, for rest or reflection among old friends.

Sir John Betjeman, much loved poet of churchyards, obviously had a great affection for God's Acre:

> For churchyards then, though hallowed ground
> Were not so grim as now they sound,
> And horns of ale were handed round
> For which churchwardens used to pay
> On each especial vestry day.
> 'Twas thus the village drunk its beer
> With its relations buried near,
> And that is why we often see
> Inns where the alehouse used to be
> Close to the church where prayers were said
> And Masses for the village dead.
>
> But this I know, you're sure to find
> Some headstones of the Georgian kind
> In each old churchyard near and far,
> Just go and see how fine they are.
> Notice the lettering of that age
> Spaced like a noble title-page,
> The parish names cut deep and strong
> To hold the shades of evening long,
> The quaint and sometimes touching rhymes
> By parish poets of the times,
> Bellows, or reaping hook or spade
> To show perhaps the dead man's trade,
> And cherubs in the corner spaces
> With wings and English ploughboy faces ...

*Churchyards*

# History of the Churchyard

For thousands of years, long before the arrival of Christianity or the Romans, the burial of the dead and the rituals associated with it have been taking place all over the country. In Gloucestershire ancient pagan burial sites such as long barrows, stone circles and standing stones have been dated to as far back as 3000 BC. A tomb was considered simply to be a house for the dead, and the grave goods which often accompanied the corpse were an indication that there was religious or mystical belief in an after-life. The area is rich in prehistoric standing stones and circles, the Rollright Stones being perhaps the most famous. The standing stones at Minchinhampton and Staunton are both possible markers for Bronze Age cemeteries.

The first individual monuments date from the Roman occupation and were known as *stelae*. In Cirencester museum are two Roman headstones from the first century AD which were found in Watermoor in 1835-6, both carved from local limestone and showing the mounted soldiers in battle, their names and ages inscribed beneath. By Roman law the burial of the dead over the age of 40 days was forbidden within the town defences. Until the second century cremation was the customary form of disposal but burial became common from the third century onwards. Their cemeteries were rectangular and orderly, the dead being place in wooden coffins, although the wealthy had covered stone coffins of which there are two in the museum.

With the spread of Christianity over the third and fourth centuries many of the new converts clung to their pagan origins, establishing the early Christian sites within previously pagan boundaries which were then purified and dedicated to the Christian faith. Even those who had mixed feelings about the new religion were more likely to accept it on a spot they already considered to be sacred. Circular churchyards such as those at Ozleworth and Hewelsfield are known to be very ancient pagan sites.

There is no doubt that many churchyards are much older than even the earliest wooden churches that stood on them. The earliest signs of the Christian faith were wooden or stone crosses which were erected, often on previously pagan sites, to mark the place for the purpose of religious instruction and worship. The Lypiatt Cross, of which only the shaft remains, is an 8th century teaching cross which stands by the road from Bisley to Stroud. Priests travelled out from monastic houses which were centres of religious worship to preach, to celebrate mass and to baptise converts to the new faith. Makeshift altars were placed in front of the crosses until the worshippers built a permanent one and enclosed it in a simple log hut. It was a natural progression to build some sort of shelter for themselves, and so in approximately the sixth century the first church buildings were born. In 601 AD Pope Gregory sent word to his missionaries that pagan temples were not to be destroyed, but were to be converted to the new faith.

It was in AD 752 that St. Cuthbert was granted permission by the Pope to establish churchyards around churches, thus ensuring that

**Plate 1**. *Standing stone at Minchinhampton*

the living were reminded of their own mortality and that Masses were said for the dead, supposedly to speed their passage through Purgatory. Churchyards varied in size, their cardinal points marked by wooden crosses. It was not until after the Norman Conquest that a system of parishes developed; until then priests travelled out from monastic houses or minsters which were the centres of religious life. Gradually daughter churches were built and wealthy landowners began to build churches on their own land. A number of churches still stand in the lee of great houses, such as Badminton, Astall, and Ozleworth, which has a particular charm of its own. It stands in what is almost the back yard of Ozleworth Park, although the church has been there six hundred years longer than the present house.

In the 10th century the practice of enclosing one acre was introduced, the origin of the name 'God's Acre.' From earliest times the area surrounding the church has been considered a sanctuary to which people could flee when danger threatened. Pagan symbols and beliefs were still not far below the surface: the ceremony of 'Clipping the Church' which takes place every year at Painswick is thought to be a relic of a pagan ritual.

At first only priests were buried in the churchyard, but perhaps because of a desire to lie close to their spiritual leaders, gradually lay members of the congregation were also allowed to be buried there. The area to the south of the church is where the oldest graves are to be found; the choice of the sunny side may reflect the pagan worship of the sun-god. The north side, in the shadow of the church, was reserved for suicides, criminals, strangers and unbaptised babies. There were no churchyard memorials: anyone rich enough to have a monument erected would be buried inside the church.

The churchyard became a centre of community life, almost like the village hall of today. Hogarth's contemporary picture of The Idle 'Prentice at Play in the Churchyard During Divine Service' shows a group of youths gambling on top of a chest tomb, surrounded by grinning skulls and human bones. Fairs and markets were held, travelling pedlars sold their wares, musicians played. Livestock were bought and sold, games played, all of which helped augment the priest's income. 'Church ales' were held on feast days to raise money for the poor and for repairs to the church, until they were eventually superseded by the introduction of parish rates.

On the parapet of Cirencester church are thirty-eight carvings known as the Whitsun Ale Procession: stone figures are shown playing

**Figure 1.** *Tombstone from first century A.D to the Roman soldier Dannicus. (Drawing by N Griffiths)*

musical instruments with the injunction to 'be merry.'

The porch was considered to be the place for serious business, for taking oaths and settling disputes. The room above the porch at Northleach was the living quarters of the priest. At Oddington there are marks on the stone benches in the porch showing where archers sharpened their arrows. During the Civil War the churchyards of Cirencester, Painswick and Stow were used as prisons, and prisoners were executed in the churchyard at Burford in 1649.

Throughout the Middle Ages the wealthy had elaborate memorials erected inside the church; outside the poor were buried in simple shrouds in a hole in the ground, without a coffin. The body would be laid on its back facing east on an east/west alignment, another relic of pagan worship of the sun-god. Burials would start at one end of the churchyard and when the burial ground was full they would go back to the beginning and start again. Eventually there would be two or more layers of bones in very shallow graves, and it became necessary to remove some of them to the crypt or charnel house in the church. In several ancient churchyards there is such an accumulation of bodies that the surface of the ground has been raised several feet, and a channel has had to be cut around the church for drainage purposes. Kenneth Lindley calculated in 'Of Graves and Epitaphs' that a twelfth-century churchyard with only six burials a year would by now contain some 4,800 bodies. There are good examples of raised churchyards at Newnham, Awre and Idbury.

At Coaley and at Newland there are still visible traces of a burial path, by which bodies were brought to the church from outlying hamlets. In Coaley the parish bier is still in the churchyard shed.

Churchyards as we know them today are post-Reformation. The early tombs which survive are often crudely cut with primitive lettering; interesting ones are to be found in several of our churchyards, including Broadwell(1601) Miserden(1605) and Standish(1639). By the beginning of the seventeenth century the wealth of the middle classes was increasing and more people could afford a memorial. The period from 1700 — 1850 produced the finest churchyard monuments such a those at Painswick, Burford and Elmore.

The nineteenth century and the Industrial Revolution saw a rise in population which created problems of overcrowding for city churchyards and to a lesser extent for country churchyards. Grave robbing became a profitable business and it was said that at St Eadburgh's Church near Broadway it was the son of the drunken parson who led the gang. As much as £20 was reputedly paid by medical schools for a 'good clean corpse' as improvements in surgical techniques created a demand for bodies for dissection; the heavy ledger stones which are still common today were a deterrent to body-snatchers, as was the practice of surrounding the grave with iron railings.

With churchyards becoming increasingly foul and unhygienic the Burial Act of 1852 allowed for cemeteries to be set up to accommodate the increased number of burials. They were established by local authorities in the same way as drains and water supplies, to meet the urgent need caused by large population migration into the cities. To this day they have little of the character of churchyards: few mature trees, with none of the pleasing mellowness of local stone. The modern cemetery full of foreign stones and polished marbles set in regimented rows is the result of the improvements in transport and the rise of the monumental mason. Cremation, which only became legal in 1884, has brought a more recent fashion to the churchyard: small cremation plaques which line the path or form a Garden of Remembrance.

# Folklore

To many people a churchyard is still a place that arouses vague feelings of unease, of supernatural happenings and ghosts rising from the grave. To our ancestors death was the ultimate mystery, wrapped in superstitions and rituals that were left over from pagan times.

A churchyard that is a restful, pleasant place by day feels very different at night, as William Shakespeare wrote in 'Hamlet:'

'Tis now the very witching time of night,
When churchyards yawn, and hell itself
   breathes out
Contagion to this world.'

The opening scene of Dickens' Great Expectations' describes the churchyard as a 'bleak place' in which the unfortunate Pip was set upon by the convict Magwitch. He watched him lumber off through the churchyard 'as if he were eluding the hands of the dead people, stretching up cautiously out of their graves, to get a twist upon his ankle and pull him in.'

Even in the modern society of today tales of the occult, of witches and ghosts and evil spirits are not far below the surface. In the village of Ilmington, off the north east corner of the Cotswolds the ghost of William Golding, Parish Clerk who died in 1763, is said to haunt the churchyard at midnight. Here too a ghostly night coach driven by six horses and followed by a pack of phantom hounds, travels along the churchyard wall.

The Devil was the image of Death personified, and while he was believed to be excluded from the church itself it was thought that he existed in the churchyard. Gargoyles and grotesques on the church wall were designed to keep evil spirits away; coins or stones were placed on the eyes of the dead because it was thought that evil spirits escaped through the eye sockets, and the heavy stones laid over graves were also intended to prevent the escape of evil spirits.

There has long been a superstition that the Devil lingers on the north side of the church. In mediaeval times only beggars, criminals and illegitimate children were buried on the north side. To this day coffins are taken from the church at North Cerney by the north door, a relic of an ancient superstition.

The belief that bodies once buried should remain undisturbed is sometimes reflected in the epitaph on the tombstone. There is one at Sapperton to Sarah, daughter of John and Elizabeth Whining who died 16th April 1795, an infant nine months old:

Move not these bones till that awful Tribunal
When you as well as they will appear to give
   Account
Of thought, words and actions at all times in
   all Places and upon all occasions.

There is a legend in Uley about a veteran of the Peninsular Wars who could remember a skeleton being found in a ditch near his home. It was believed to be that of a Scottish pedlar who had disappeared, probably murdered, some time before. It was taken up to the church and laid in the porch on Sundays. The superstition held that if the man who murdered him came by, the skeleton would bleed.

Although at one time it was common practice to graze sheep and goats in the churchyard, I heard an old wives' tale recently that may be local to Gloucestershire.

'Animals grazed in the churchyard go thin,' I was told. 'And if you cut the churchyard for hay nobody won' buy 'un, for them animals as is fed on 'un, they'll go thin.'

Evergreens and yew trees in particular have been a part of the folklore of the churchyard since pagan times. Because it lives to a great age the yew tree is seen as the symbol of immortality, older than any other living thing, the fountain of ancient wisdom, the keeper of the secrets of life itself. In fact yew trees may have achieved their importance because they were there first; being evergreen they provided shelter for the early Christian missionaries and the church was built on the site of the yew tree, not the other way round. In mediaeval times branches of evergreen were laid on the coffin or body bag to ward off evil spirits and as a symbol of immortality; their red cupped berries were regarded as drops of blood.

# The Setting

If there is one thing that a churchyard has that a cemetery lacks it is an atmosphere, a 'feel'. It contains more than just a collection of memorials to the dead; there are gates and boundaries; trees and hedges, plants, lichens and mosses; out there among the tilting stones there may be a whole hidden world of wildlife, of birds and insects, foxes and squirrels.

Stand for a moment at the entrance; what is the feel of this churchyard? Is it loved and cared for, perhaps by one or two devoted parishioners? Is it waist high in nettles and brambles, the tombs covered in ivy? Or is it mown as smooth as a billiard table, the headstones cleared to the boundary or worse still, broken and discarded in a heap in the corner?

There are some churchyards where the whole setting is perfection. Bibury, where the church, the stones and the surrounding buildings blend together in a harmony of mellow stone. Painswick, best known of all, where the elegant spire dominates the famous churchyard with its ninety nine yews.

The most picture-postcard setting must be the Eastleaches, where two churches face each other across the river Leach, spanned by John Keble's clapper bridge, the meadows full of nodding daffodils in spring. Or Westwell, named from the most western spring in Oxfordshire, which has everything: manor house, village green, duck-pond complete with ducks and moorhens, mullioned houses in the rich golden stone of the eastern Cotswolds. A Bronze Age henge or circle once stood in a field close to the village, and a Saxon chapel is thought to have been sited by the spring.

**Plate 2**. *Lassington Tower*

**Plate 3**. *Gargoyles and wolves on Compton Abdale tower*

There are others, less well known, each with its own particular attraction. Sometimes the position of the church is so spectacular as to be breathtaking; the odd-looking church at Selsley, famous for its William Morris stained glass, sits perched on the side of the western scarp over the Stroud valley, spectacular from above or below. At the other end of the Cotswolds the old church at Saintbury with its tall landmark spire looks out above the village over a panorama of blue and distant views. Or Ruardean, where the churchyard seems to be poised above the Wye, the woodland of the Forest burnished red and gold in the autumn sun.

Sometimes the setting is unexpected. In Cirencester, yards from the town centre and the tourist traffic the churchyard is tucked away beside the parish church, a green oasis of peace and tranquillity in the middle of a busy town.

Quite different, yet just as surprising, is St Oswald's Tower, all that is left of the church at Lassington, west of Gloucester. Here at the end of a narrow lane there is total silence apart from the birds, and another sloping churchyard with excellent headstones in Forest stone, still legible after nearly 300 years.

Off the beaten track are the secret places with a feel all of their own. Syde, on the slopes of the Frome valley, is one of the oldest and smallest parishes in England. It was an ancient Saxon settlement and the south doorway has a heavy, rough-cut lintel of Saxon style. One complete side of the churchyard is taken up by a great 14th century tithe barn which gives the little churchyard a feeling of privacy and seclusion. It was once the centre of local commercial activity, a collection house for the fleeces and crops which were destined for the great Abbeys of Gloucester and Cirencester. At the lower end of the barn is a little dwelling known as the Priest's House, and the priest referred to in the Domesday Book may well have lived here.

At Boxwell the road descends through ancient woods to open out suddenly into a hidden valley, a hamlet of only a few houses with dry-stone walls and spilling flowers. The little church with its 13th century bellcote sits snugly close to the manor house, the sloping churchyard almost a part of the garden, its large classical chest tomb rich in symbolic carving and lichens.

And Ashley, close to the Wiltshire border, where the little church is almost lost among the stone walls and great barns of Manor Farm. The churchyard is as neat as a new pin without looking overmown or cultivated, its flagstones paths paved with old ledger stones, a few of the inscriptions still legible in parts.

**Plate 4**. *Bellcote at Little Badminton*

The smallest churchyard of all must be at Edge: not the Victorian church on the main road but the now disused Congregational Chapel on the village green. Next to it is a triangle of grass smaller than the average duckpond, containing two memorials, one to Henry Tilling, the other to William James Steele, the last preacher at the chapel. He died in June 1967, and a few people in the village remember him as a portly, bespectacled figure. The little graveyard is lovingly maintained by the couple who now own the chapel.

Then there are the places that have some particular, indefinable quality that makes them unforgettable. Compton Abdale is one of these: the church stands on a hill high above the gabled roofs of the village; on the pinnacles of the tower are strange heraldic beasts thought to be either Warwick bears or wolves or dogs from the Howe family who lived nearby. The buttress offsets are decorated with couchant Cotswold rams, a sure indication that the church was built with wool money. In the churchyard is a very old chest tomb with the remains of a carved head on the lid and also a little headstone only 18 inches high

**Plate 5**. *Church in a field — Ampney St Mary*

with a raised edge and a very badly carved inscription written in the wrong order. It reads:

Here lieth the body of John Wilson O Lord I will (sic)arias and go to my Father at the last day who died ?1735.

In this churchyard we found an orange hawkweed flower holding its head above the grass, presumably escaped from a garden.

The steep ascent must surely create problems for the elderly and infirm; for those who can't manage it there is a seat at the bottom where the spring gushes out of the mouth of a stone crocodile, complete with teeth, into a great stone trough below.

At the other end of the Cotswolds is Little Badminton, an unexpectedly large churchyard for such a small village, with mature trees and some nice nineteenth century headstones. The church was sadly shut, with two sheaves of corn leaning against the wall waiting hopefully for the Harvest Festival. It looks more like a barn than a church, until you see the bell beneath a bracket at the west end and beside it a single carved

grotesque of a man's head, his fingers on his cheeks as though propping up his head. At his feet as though he is reading it is a raised ledger describing the sad end of William Eels:

To the cherished memory of William Eels
Born October 27 1827
Accidently killed January 14th 1851
Who must but shed a tear
When they behold the sad end of one who possessed those qualities fitted to adorn the highest station.
His active ardent mind elate, so gracious and sincere
No thought that ill did him await
Nor did he yield to fear.
But slippery was the path he trod
And dangerous the way
For whilst the deer did him surround
They did his horse betray.
How sacred is this hallowed spot
To sorrowing friends and sister dear
Who feels the loss of an only brother
Beloved by all through life's career.

For atmosphere there is nothing to beat those churches where the population has moved away. It may have been because of the Black Death, or changes in economic conditions, or as with Kempley, because the old church was subject to flooding and a new one was built on higher ground. The church at Ampney St Mary was abandoned after the Black Death in 1439, and now stands quite alone in a meadow. Until its restoration in 1913 it was known locally as the Ivy Church. It has some good chest tombs, and the churchyard cross appears to be carved in one piece from the tree which forms the base. Over the north door is a rare treasure, a carved lintel with a twelfth century sculpture showing a griffin and the Lion of Righteousness trampling evil spirits.

At Frocester only the tower remains. Ralph Bigland in his tremendous work recording the churchyards of Gloucestershire in the eighteenth century writes:

> The ancient village is said to have been contiguous to the church, but having been destroyed by fire was re-established at the Distance of a Mile from it, upon the great Road from Gloucester to Bath from the former of which this place is the first commodious stage.

The stone was sold to build the church at Wycliffe College, but the churchyard is still in use and well cared for, with wild flowers showing their heads among the stones.

And finally there is Bagpath. Alone above the Newington valley the church is disused and boarded up, but the churchyard contains two gravestones to the (sic)Shakespear family, including one that is supposedly that of the last known relative of William Shakespeare. Here there is total quietude; no traffic, no human voice; only the birds and the wind in the tall beech trees break the eerie silence.

# Lychgates and Boundaries

A number of churchyards including Frocester are approached through a lychgate, a roofed structure whose original purpose was to provide shelter for the pall bearers and the coffin while they waited for the arrival of the priest to conduct the procession. The word is derived from the Anglo-Saxon word *lich* for corpse. In mediaeval times they would have had a central bench, or coffin stone to rest the coffin on. Since they were made of wood, few of these have survived, although there is a modern coffin stone in the lychgate dated 1917 at Kington St Michael on the Wiltshire slopes of the Cotswolds.

One of the oldest lychgates is at Painswick; it is made out of old timbers from the belfry, weathered to a silvery grey. Its bargeboards are carved with bells, with stone benches flanking the sides.

Most of the lychgates have been erected as a memorial, either to an individual or to the fallen in the two World Wars. The one at Badgeworth has intricate carving, including a staff of music with the words O rest in the Lord, and was erected in 1910 in memory of Jane Unwin by her six children. There are interesting ones at Charlton Kings and at Dymock, where the bargeboards are decorated with grapes and vine leaves with the figure of St Michael in the gable.

The little lychgate at Duntisbourne Rouse opens on to a grassy walk between green hedges, a most attractive approach to this Norman church with its saddleback tower. So steep is the sloping churchyard that there was room for a crypt to be built beneath the chancel, which is approached by steps from the churchyard. At Duntisbourne Abbotts, just along the valley there

**Plate 6**. *Lychgate at Dymock*

**Plate 7**. *Swing gate at Duntisbourne Abbotts*

is a revolving lychgate, designed to make the passage of the coffin easier, and nowadays a great temptation to young children. There is also a revolving one at North Cerney, sheltered by stately beech and sycamore trees. At Lydney there is a sundial perched on top of the lychgate, and at Leonard Stanley the lychgate is more recent, solidly built and well designed.

Where the churchyard gates are made of wrought iron they are often worth a second glance as good examples of local craftsmanship. Often there is an arched bracket above to take a lamp. The little gate into the churchyard at St Andrew's, Awre, has St A set into the design. In the two villages of Clapton-on-the-Hill and Farmington, high in the Cotswolds above Northleach the churchyard gates are made from horseshoes; presumably the work of a local blacksmith. Perhaps the shoes had covered a few miles round the lanes before coming to rest as part of the church gate.

One of the great differences between a churchyard and a more recent cemetery or churchyard extension, as they are sometimes known, is the absence of mature trees. Where they form the boundary they provide a windbreak, sheltering visitors and wildlife as well as the fabric of the church and its gravestones. There are stately rows of trees at Elkstone, Broadwell and Haresfield, and surely the magnificent beeches which are so much a part of the atmosphere at Lechlade must have led Percy Bysshe Shelley to write in 1815:

Here could I hope
that death did hide from human sight
sweet secrets..

Trees lend character and shape; some of the yew trees in the county are anything up to 1,500 years old, and it is noticeable that where they shelter tombstones, as at Haresfield and Sapperton, the inscriptions and carvings are well preserved. The row of limes in Dymock churchyard marks the route of a Roman road which in mediaeval times was the village street. In the churchyard at Duntisbourne Abbotts there is a beautiful beech tree, where a woman tending her husband's grave told me that there were so many beech nuts on the ground the previous autumn that they blocked the cutters of the mower.

In a churchyard like Painswick where yew trees line the paths they are an integral part of the character, adding colour and depth to the setting of the church so that without them the nature of the churchyard would be completely different. Kings Stanley is another where trimmed yews line the path; at Miserden there is

# Memory of

a splendid yew arch, and at Brimpsfield, a church across a field, there are three, one after the other, as you walk up the path.

The church at Hawkesbury Upton is down a steep narrow lane almost off the edge of the Cotswolds near the Avon border. The outside of this handsome church has a number of interesting features, including a sundial on the south porch and a thirteenth century coffin lid built into the wall. Here the tall hedge of yews that forms the boundary has been trimmed square, reflecting the castellated parapet above.

**Plate 8**. *Horseshoe gate at Clapton-on-the-Hill*

**Plate 9**. *Norman doorway, Windrush*

The grand boundary wall at Selsley had a large oval opening with wrought iron letters, presumably so that the church can be seen from the house next door. And several churchyards have cottages forming the boundary, like Elkstone and Blockley, where the interested eyes of the windows seem to be peering out over the gravestones in mild curiosity.

**Plate 10.** *Dumbleton tympanum*

# Exteriors

The outside of the church is as much a part of the churchyard as the gravestones, the trees and the boundaries. The church itself can make the churchyard attractive or forbidding, for the masonry, the doorways, the carvings are the backdrop to the gravestones and part of the 'feel' of the whole.

There are a few places where the outside of the church is so splendid that the eye is drawn to it like a magnet and visitors walk up the path without a glance at what is almost at their feet. The great 'wool' churches have this effect: the magnificent pinnacled and crocketed porch at Northleach, the imposing Perpendicular tower of Chipping Campden. The south porch at Malmesbury is outstanding, described by Denis Moriarty as 'one of the most important sculptural ensembles in England.' Even in some of our little churches are reminders that the porch has an important function in modern parish life: a place for shelter and for the exchange of information. In the porch at Duntisbourne Rouse there is a reminder of the difficulties faced by small parishes these days: a notice asking for support says that there are only thirty parishioners, of which nearly half are children or pensioners.

A number of the porches that shelter Norman doorways are younger than the church and have provided protection against the weather for carvings and tympani over the doorways. The famous Norman tympanum at Elkstone is one of the best known, the work of its mediaeval stone carvings still sharp after eight hundred years. Of the same period are the two doorways at Quenington; the south one depicts the Coronation of the Virgin in a chevron moulding, while the north doorway shows the Harrowing of Hell surrounded by four ranks of elaborate mouldings, the outer one continuing down the jambs of the doorway. At Windrush the south door is unprotected by a porch; it has a double row of beakheads with bulging eyes glaring at the beautiful chest tomb opposite.

Over the doorway at Dumbleton, on one of the northern outliers of the Cotswolds the tympanum has carved capitals and a zigzag arch, it

**Plate 11**. *Shears on 15th century tower at Cranham (Geoffrey N Wright)*

shows an extraordinary comical figure of a man with the ears of an ass and foliage sticking out of his mouth. There are worn grotesques keeping him company along the string course, looking out over two very old chest tombs in yellow stone with inset panels and pilasters on the corners.

Another Norman tympanum at Little Barrington has been moved to the outside north wall, showing Christ in Majesty flanked by angels, their wings forming a protective canopy. On the outside of the porch wall is a group of four stone figures in bold relief showing four little girls, one pair in bonnets and holding hands, the other pair in long cloaks. It is a memorial to the Tayler family; the inscription reads:

Neare this Place lyeth ye body of William Tayler Snr who was buryed May ye 14 1699 aged 45 years and alsoe William Tayler Jnr who was buried October 3 1702 aged 21 years. Also Elizabeth Tayler ye wife of William Tayler who was buryed January ye 28 1727 aged 78 years. Mary the wife of William Mury, daughter of William and Elizabeth Tayler, departed this life November ye 11 1733 aged 49 Years, 4 months and 8 days.

There are external plaques also at Ampney Crucis and at Selsley, where the memorial to Sir Samuel Marling, benefactor of the church, is built into the south wall.

The best known exterior must be the one at North Cerney, where there is another Norman doorway, for here there are incised drawings on the south transept and the tower. They are supposed to represent the odd creatures which the Roman writer, Pliny, called manticores. One is a beast with the body and legs of a dog with small hooves and the face of a man, and is over four feet long. The other also has a man's face with the body of a leopard and a long tail. David Verey dates them as post-Reformation, perhaps the doodles of some local mason.

Hidden away off the main road from Tetbury to Dursley is the little hamlet of Beverston, a gem in Cotswold stone. There are stone finials on the gables of the cottages, supposedly to stop the devil resting there and the ruin of Beverston castle stands in massive dignity in a beautiful garden. The Norman church has four coffin covers incised with floreated crosses built into the north wall, and on the south face of the tower is a worn pre-Conquest figure of Christ in high relief, the right hand raised in benediction, the resurrection banner in the left. At Ashley the west window has a lintel carved from a stone coffin lid.

The church at Cranham is not noted as one of the great 'wool' churches, but high on the wall of the fifteenth century tower two pairs of shears are carved, perhaps indicating that the tower was built with money donated by a wool merchant.

The masonry in the porch at Daglingworth includes Saxon short-and -long work, evidence of the great age of this little church, as is the Saxon sundial over the entrance. Set into the floor is a brass plate in beautiful script recording the generosity of a local benefactor:

Dissection and Distribution of Giles
  Hancox
Who Earthe bequeathe to Earth to Heaven
  his Soul
To Friends his Love
To the Poore a Five Pound Dole
To remain for ever and be Employed
For their best Advantage and Reliefe in
  Daglingworth
April 9th 1638

# Blacksmith

This church contains some of the best preserved Saxon carvings in the country, discovered during building work in the nineteenth century.

## Dials

Scratch or mass dials are to be seen on the south face of quite a number of churches, although they are not always easy to find. Among the oldest, apart from Daglingworth, are Oddington, Bagendon, Saintbury and one at North Cerney which is thought to be pre-Conquest. They consist of a rough circle cut into the stone with incised lines radiating from a central hole. The radiating lines may indicate the times of the church services rather than the time of day, the deepest lines showing the time of the most

important mass. The metal pin, or gnomon, from which the shadow fell will have long since disappeared, leaving a splayed hole.

There is an eighteenth century four-sided sundial on a nineteenth century base at Upton St Leonards, and at Charlton Kings the head of an old sundial sits on a more recent pillar. The one at Brimpsfield is dated Trafalgar Year, and just inside the lychgate at Minchinhampton is a sundial on a memorial, now sadly vandalised. South Cerney and Naunton have painted dials on the tower, both in good condition.

But the last word must go to a more recent lead sundial at Dumbleton on which is inscribed:
WASTE ME NOT

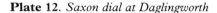

**Plate 12**. *Saxon dial at Daglingworth*

**Plate 13**. *Painted sundial at Naunton*

# Gargoyles

If we needed proof that the masons of our mediaeval masons had a sense of humour we need
only to look at the gargoyles and grotesques that
adorn our churches. They are everywhere: over
doorways and string courses, on towers and
parapets, on hood moulds and dripstones. They
are funny and sad, pathetic or grim, and they
portray every imaginable sort of mythical
creature, animal and human being. Both Coates
and Coaley have a gruesome fifteenth century
anthropophagus consuming his victim.

Strictly speaking, gargoyles are water spouts,
built outwards from the gutter or the side of the
church to throw the rainwater clear of the building. Grotesques seem to be purely decorative,

**Plate 14.** *Grotesques at Winchcombe*

**Plate 15.** *Ashleworth mediaeval cross*

and are often found in a series along a string
course, like the ones at Elkstone and Fairford.
They were undoubtably meant to represent the
forces of evil and to warn the local population of
the temptations of the devil. They may have had
their origins in ancient legends and folk-tales.

Some of the largest and best are at Aldsworth,
where there is an empty decorated niche set into
the north east corner, and above it a huge
bearded head with hands holding a scourge. All
along the string course just below the parapet is a
series of large grotesques of gaping and grimac-
ing faces with staring eyes, dragons, animals and
an unusual beakhead with a roll-moulding in its
mouth, probably copied from a Norman doorway.

There are about forty grotesques at Winchcombe on the porch, the clerestory and the parapets, some of them looking so human that they
must surely be caricatures of local people. One of
them is a winged man in a battered top hat, his
face twisted as though in pain; there are also
demons, monkeys and a jester, leering down at
the modern traffic as it squeezes through this
narrow little town.

There are also outstanding collections of
grotesques and gargoyles at Chedworth, Barnsley
and Willersey. Many smaller churches such as

Naunton, Coaley, Eastleach St Martin and Kings Stanley have gargoyles on the tower. Those at Fairford and Elkstone are dealt with in a later chapter.

# In the Grounds

The churchyard itself can contain a great deal of interest apart from the gravestones, and sometimes a few surprises. The churches at Berkeley and Westbury both have detached towers, which in the country as a whole are not uncommon. The one at Berkeley is several hundred years younger than the church, and is built on the base of a previous tower by the gate. At Westbury the tower is much older; it was built in 1270 as a garrison tower and was besieged by both sides in turn during the Civil War.

Originally every churchyard would have had a cross, either an ancient pagan stone re-dedicated to the new religion, or a cross erected by the new Christian missionaries to mark a preaching station. During the Middle Ages the cross would have been the sole memorial to all those unmarked graves in the churchyard, but during the Reformation a great number were destroyed. Not many remain intact in this part of the country although there is a fourteenth century Maltese cross in a circle at North Cerney. At Ampney Crucis there is a restored mediaeval cross with a gabled head and sculptures showing a Madonna and St John. It survived the iconoclasts by being walled up and hidden inside the church.

The cross in the riverside village of Ashleworth has now been moved to the village green. It has a lantern head and four niches sheltering a Crucifixion with two women kneeling to a Madonna. The one at Duntisbourne Rouse is also fourteenth century, although the head is very worn. A number of churchyards have remnants of mediaeval crosses, usually a headless shaft on a stepped base, including Daglingworth, Harescombe, Eastleach St Martin and Cheltenham. At Ampney St Mary the wooden cross appears to have been cut recently from the trunk of a standing tree, perhaps the remains one of the cedars which used to shelter the north side.

The churchyard can also contain the unexpected, like the tip of the spire at Stroud, which was removed during the last century after it was damaged by lightning. In several churchyards there are old stone coffins, and at Winchcombe and Kington St Michael they have been put to good use as flower-troughs. Outside the north doorway at Syde is a thirteenth century grave cover with an incised cross. Just outside the gate at Ashley there are mounting-steps, a relic of the days when people came to church on horseback.

**Plate 16**. *Stocks at Painswick Church*

Outside the church wall at Painswick are the village stocks, well painted and looking ready for use. At Saintbury and Dymock there are dole tables — stone slabs or tombs which have been used for distributing money or bread to the local poor, usually bequeathed by wealthy patrons. In the excellent illustrated leaflet from Dymock church there is the comment that this is one way to get your congregation to church on a Sunday!

Churchyards have their people too, that army of willing volunteers who mow the grass, weed the paths and tend the graves. A gentleman at Coates was having his photograph taken when I was there; he was the winner of the competition for the best kept churchyard, which was his pride and joy. It was certainly meticulous; each grave was trimmed around the edge, the grass was neatly cut to the bottom of the Cotswold walls and there was not a sprig of ivy in sight. In an accent as thick as custard he leaned on his rake to tell me he had looked after it man and boy for fifty years.

Then there was the man feeding the ducks at Westwell, his face weathered by the Cotswold winds, his trousers hanging loose from leather braces. His eye swept disdainfully over the tidy, lifeless houses round the village green. "I used to do the churchyard," he said, "But them's taken it off me with their fancy machines." And he clanked away with his bucket, the ducks squawking round his feet.

Many of the more modest churches have individual features that are just as attractive; I like to think that the people who have made it what it is, the masons, labourers, clergymen, are among those who lie at peace in the churchyard under the benevolent eye of the church.

# Memorials

Memorials come in all shapes and sizes, from the strictly functional, bearing a simple record of the deceased, to the ostentatious or even eccentric. From plain horizontal slabs, or ledgers to a variety of carved headstones and finally to the chest or table tomb, which can be anything from a plain unadorned box to an intricately carved and ornate memorial to some wealthy and important personage. Gloucestershire has the greatest concentration of chest tombs in the country, with the most outstanding of the best at Standish, Haresfield, Painswick and Elmore.

## Headstones

The headstone is a natural progression from the *stelae* of the pre-Christian era. The oldest that survive in our churchyards today are seventeenth century, small squat stones, thick in relation to their height and two feet or less in height. They have an inset inner panel with the inscription carved somewhat erratically in the available space. There must be hundreds of these little stones that have sunk beneath the soil over the years. Of those that have survived there are well-preserved ones at Newland, Awre and Woolstone as well as individual ones in a number of churchyards.

The eighteenth century saw headstones becoming larger and thinner, with the top edge or *hood* being carved into more ornate shapes. Later it began to incorporate curves, scrolls, and angel heads. There are good ones at Astall and Taynton, and Brimpsfield also has a pleasing collection well colonised by lichens. In the charming collection at Swinbrook the angels that make up the hood moulds look as though they are wearing ear-muffs, with stone scrolls close to their faces. As often happens, there is a similarity here

**Plate 17.** *17th century stone at Newland*

among the headstones of a churchyard or group of churchyards which indicates the work of one man. This is particularly noticeable at Bibury, almost self-conscious in its perfection, where the uniformity of stone colouring and texture makes the churchyard one with its surroundings.

With the influence of classical art and the refinement of design towards the middle of the eighteenth century the hood again became plainer while the sculptor turned his attention to the face of the stone. The inscription would be placed inside a decorated shield or *cartouche* surrounded by foliage and flowers. Sometimes the face of the stone would be divided vertically to carry two inscriptions side by side.

Forest of Dean stone has survived the passage of time far better than the Cotswold limestone.

Carvings and inscriptions are well preserved over a wide area, with good collections particularly at Longney and Lassington. On the fringes of the Forest Lydney is outstanding, and there are beautiful stones at Ruardean, Minsterworth, Newland and English Bicknor. Multiple angel heads were evidently the speciality of a local mason: on a headstone at Newnham-on-Severn there are thirteen, a sad reminder of the child mortality rate in the eighteenth century. The inscription reads:

> In memory of Susannah the wife of James
> Drew of the parish of Littledean who
> died February 10th 1796 aged 41 years.
> Also two of their children Phebe and
> Emanuel were here buried.
>
> Farewel deare husband whom I leave
> behind
> And children five tho much against my
> mind
> My glass is run God thought it best
> To take me to eternal rest.
> Also James and Sarah Fillips, parents of the
> above Susan Drew and nine of their
> sons here buried.

The foot of the grave was often marked by a smaller footstone. Not many of these remain; those that do may have been moved to stand back-to-back with the headstone. The footstone was usually inscribed just with the initials to cor-

**Plate 18.** *'Angel top' stone at Littledean*

**Plate 19.** *'Angel top' stone with book at Sapperton*

respond with the headstone and perhaps the date. At Beverston there is a footstone inscribed with the initials SH and a skull and crossbones, a great rarity.

The late eighteenth and early nineteenth century brought a uniformity of stone in shape and size, usually with a larger panel on which the stonemason could demonstrate the emerging skills of letter-cutting. The decoration would be confined mostly to the top, incorporating all the symbols of mortality and eternity which were then fashionable: cherubs, angels, draped urns, books and hourglasses. Headstones of this period are to be seen everywhere, and Inglesham, Shilton, Windrush and Winchcombe are well worth a visit. At Awre there is a whole row of them lining the path, many of them 'doubles', showing winged cherubs all with a certain similarity as though they were brothers.

Sometimes the carving can be almost biographical, like the memorial to William Keyes, a blacksmith, at Frampton-on-Severn who died in 1795. It shows that he was a musician as well; there are musical instruments including a violin and a French horn with sheet music. It is the

**Plate 20**. *Late 18th century stone at Lydney*

**Plate 21**. *Twin inscriptions on a stone at Tetbury*

work of John Pierce, a well known local mason whose trade mark was a drooping sheaf of foliage.

Across the river in the churchyard at Westbury-on-Severn is a grey stone portrait of William Clarke, a schoolmaster who died in 1835. He is shown sitting at his desk in a wide-skirted coat and breeches, writing with a quill pen. Around him are artists' materials, books and plumbers tools, showing him to be a man of wide interests.

At Broadway an eighteenth century headstone shows barbers' tools scattered among winged cherubs with flowing locks, while at Eastington, on the outskirts of Stroud is a memorial to another blacksmith, William Howell, who died in 1825 aged eighty-five. In between pineapples growing out of urns is a funny little structure that is undoubtably his forge.

# Ledgers

Historically, horizontal slabs or ledgers are almost as old as headstones. At South Cerney there is an enormous lidded Saxon coffin of a phenomenal weight and two decorated coffin lids which were found on the site of a Saxon burial ground. In the churchyard at Bagendon is a coped Norman tomb-slab; inside the church at Brimpsfield are three decorated mediaeval tombstones which were removed from the churchyard in 1970. Ledgers are common inside churches, but unfortunately the vast majority of those outside will have long since sunk beneath the soil. It was encouraging recently to hear of one that was unearthed at Newland in good condition, although it has begun to deteriorate with exposure.

A variation on the ledger is the body stone which is tapered at both ends and rounded in cross-section. Like ledgers they were an effective deterrent against body snatchers; a nice row of body stones can be seen at Upton St Leonards. To deal with the problems of encroaching vegetation some ledgers came to be raised above the ground by a foot or so, showing the enormous bulk and weight of the slabs. At Sapperton, Stroud and Painswick there are raised ledgers, many of them with brass plates. Unlike chest tombs they can have inscriptions or plates on the upper surface, like the one at Woolstone which is a memorial to the Peacey family and Baby Thomas who died in 1810 aged ten months.

## Chest Tombs

Chest or table tombs are the external equivalent of the altar tombs inside the church. They were an effective way of raising the ledger above the encroaching vegetation, and were built originally as plain stone boxes carrying an effigy of the deceased.

One of our great treasures is a chest tomb at South Cerney which has been dated at about 1370. It has a double effigy of a civilian and his wife, their hands folded across their chests. Their heads rest on two pillows, the man bare-headed, the woman with a headdress framing her face.

**Plate 22**. *19th century headstone, Little Badminton*

**Plate 23**. *Headstone to William Clarke, Westbury*

Effigies on chest tombs are rare: there is a very well preserved one now inside Newland church which was brought in from the churchyard in 1950. It is dated 1457 and shows Jenkin Wyrrall, Forester of the Fee in dress of the period, including hunting knife and horn. On a tomb at Oddington is a life-size figure of a reclining woman in a long skirt with her feet sticking out at the end. It is dated 1695, and a similar one at Bourton-on-the-Water of which not much remains is thought to be of the same date.

In any churchyard the earliest chest tombs are to be found by the south porch and date from mediaeval times. They were rectangular stone boxes decorated with cusped quatrefoils or window tracery copied from the church and were usually without inscriptions. There are very old chest tombs at Little Barrington, Fulbrook and at Astall, now sadly collapsing.

By the early seventeenth century the side panels carried inscriptions in crude lettering. The lids were thick, overhanging the slender base with chamfered or fluted edges. Some had arched panels on the sides or ends. There are good examples at Miserden, Standish, Stonehouse and Kingscote and an unusual cruciform one at Swinbrook dated 1643. There is a group of well-preserved primitive bale tombs at Broad-

well with eight kneeling figures in the panels, dated 1601-12; there are others at Evenlode and Oddington. They have a tremendous charm, a simple dignity which is a far cry from the lavish decoration which was to come later.

Chest tombs in the less affluent Forest of Dean are far fewer than elsewhere; they never reached the heights of decoration to be found in the Vale and the Cotswolds; they were plain almost to the point of austerity with simple decoration on the side panels and usually an epitaph.

As chest tombs became more common so the skill and imagination of the sculptor increased; figures with trailing scarves appeared, heads on hands, known as 'weepers'; there are nice examples of weepers at Hardwicke, Elmore, Frampton-on-Severn, Newnham and Standish.

The late seventeenth and early eighteenth century saw the development of the chest tomb into an art form for which the western Cotswolds and the Severn Vale are famous. In the churchyards of Painswick, Haresfield, Standish and Elmore are marvellous examples of the exuberance of the sculptors of the day: cherubs tastefully draped,

**Plate 24**. *Early chest tomb with overhang, Stonehouse*

**Plate 25**. *Primitive bale tomb with kneeling figures, Broadwell*

**Plate 26**. *Detail of carved tomb, Standish*

fruit, foliage and flowers. The ends were carved into lyre shapes decorated with acanthus leaves and finished in a loose coil, while the centre was filled with the classical motifs of life, death and immortality. The side panels would carry a cartouche with a decorated border of fruit and flowers, cherub heads, skulls and skeletons. There are excellent individual tombs at Badgeworth, Bourton-on-the-Water, Eastington, Stonehouse, Elkstone, Little Barrington, Northleach, and Upton St Leonards.

The churchyards of Daglingworth, Bourton-on-the-Water, Leighterton and Harescombe have portrait busts, the one at Harescombe having recently been restored. On the lyre end of a chest tomb at Longney is a carved head and shoulders of a man in a wig, also possibly a portrait.

A variation on the chest tomb is to be found at Winson where there is a group of tombs to the Bryant family in the 1790's. They are taller than

**Plate 27**. *Detail of weeper, Haresfield*

Plate 28. *Classical chest tomb, Stonehouse*

Plate 29. *Lyre end, Standish*

usual with chamfered lids and restrained decoration on side and end panels.

It was a short step from the chest tomb to the pedestal tomb, or podium, which are higher than they are long and are known affectionately as 'tea caddies'. They can be square, round, oval or hexagonal, the sides buttressed by scrolls or consoles and decorated with angel heads and cherubs. The tops can be domed with bands of decoration or mouldings, and often they are topped with a finial or urn. The best collection is at Painswick, but they are also to be found in other churchyards including Minchinhampton, Miserden, Stonehouse, Ozleworth, Inglesham, Kington St Michael and Newnham.

There was considerable abuse of churchyards in the eighteenth century and not only from the undesirable attentions of the grave-robbers. It has been suggested that chest tombs were used by thieves and smugglers to hide stolen property. As a deterrent to thieves iron railings were built round chest tombs and podia, and in time became an art form of their own. The simple and effective work of the blacksmith later became the mass-produced highly decorative style of the Victorians, who with their respect for privacy both in their homes and in their cemeteries, believed that a man should be left where he was laid to rest. They had large heavy headstones and the grave was often surrounded with cast iron railings or a stone kerb. There are railed tombs at Blockley, Saintbury and plenty in the Forest of Dean, where cast iron was plentiful. Even today nearly every churchyard has a tomb protected by iron railings.

# Bale tombs

Bale tombs are a variation of the chest tomb which is found predominantly in the eastern Cotswolds. The early or 'primitive' ones have semi-cylindrical capping stones on the upper surface which are rounded on top and narrower than the slab they sit on. Apart from Broadwell they can be found at Westwell, Dumbleton and Swinbrook, among others.

Later bale tombs have capping stones which cover the whole of the upper surface of the chest tomb. The curved top has deep grooves cut in it,

Plate 30. *Portrait tomb, Daglingworth*

either straight across or diagonally. Traditionally they are meant to represent the corded bales of cloth of the clothiers, but it seems more likely that they are taken from the hoops which covered the hearse, and over which the pall was draped. The ends of the bale were frequently recessed with a skull set in a shell or scallop. There is a magnificent one at Windrush with carved pilasters on the corners and a ram's head set in the scalloped end. Shells are an ancient symbol with classical origins which became popular again as the pilgrims' badge in the middle ages.

In the churchyard at Quenington, where all the headstones have been moved to the boundary there is a handsome pair of chest tombs which are the only ones combining both lyre and bale. They are decorated with winged angels, acanthus leaves and fruit.

There are bale tombs in a number of churchyards, including Fulbrook, Stow-on-the-Wold and Swinbrook, where there is an ornate bale tomb decorated with wreaths and coils, with a shield set into the bale end. The best are at Bibury and Burford, where some of the grander

**Plate 31**. *Square pedestal with weeper, Newnham*

tombs have embellishments on the simple bale and finials, perhaps intended to represent the candle holders on the hearse. At Astall, under the windows of the gabled Elizabethan manor house, is a Baroque bale tomb with a finial to Harming Fletcher, dated 1717. It is decorated with cherubs and foliage an the shell end on the bale contains a little head with round cheeks like a baby.

Perhaps the grandest bale tomb of all is the magnificent three-decker tomb to the Morgan family at Shipton-under-Wychwood at the foot of the Oxfordshire Cotswolds. It is intricately carved with angels, flowers and foliage. It has a rose in the bale end and an heraldic emblem with what looks like a lizard.

# Memorials Eccentric and Unusual

All over the country there are tombstones and memorials which do not follow conventional designs, and Gloucestershire and the Cotswolds are no exception. Until recently there was little control over churchyard monuments and those people who felt that an elaborate memorial was an indication of wealth or status had a free hand.

Sometimes a tomb is remarkable not because of its shape but because of what is on it. A chest tomb at Upper Cam carries a vivid picture of Farmer Parrot who was killed by his flail, supposedly because he was ploughing on a Sunday.

Odd shapes occur everywhere. In the churchyard at Cirencester is a splendid sarcophagus above a pedestal to Captain Day, who died on April 12th 1790. It is supported by great coiled scrolls and surmounted by a fluted urn. At Dymock is a tapered chest tomb on a wide base with a domed lid, topped by an elaborate stone finial with drapes and rosettes, looking like a hat in a boutique. It is the a memorial to William Day and his family, Lords of the Manor, but sadly it was overgrown with ivy, the inscription illegible. Under the trees in a corner of Tetbury churchyard is classical chest tomb surmounted

**Plate 32**. *'Tea caddy' with finial and railings, Badgeworth*

by a very unusual high four-sided 'lid' standing on knob feet, and on top of it a finial.

The mausoleum to the Guise family at Elmore is the only one in the area, and unfortunately is a ruin. It has a sad dignity about it, the paving crumbling behind a rickety fence.

Pyramids are less rare; the one at Painswick is surprisingly austere because it is a memorial to John Bryan, himself a mason responsible for some of the fine work in that churchyard. In a corner of the churchyard at Woodchester is another pyramid standing on a symbolic triangle, representing the Trinity, itself mounted on a circle of stone, for Eternity.

Churchyard memorials to animals are rare and to many would seem sacrilegious. However it would be difficult to take exception to the the small stone memorial in Fairford churchyard to Tiddles, the church cat from 1963-1980. The

**Plate 33**. *Bale tombs with lyre ends, Quenington*

**Plate 34**. *Three-decker bale tomb, Shipton-under-wychwood*

inscription to a fish at Blockley is not in the churchyard as stated by Arthur Mee, but is in the garden of the neighbouring Fish Cottage. It reads:

> In memory of the Old Fish
> Under the soil the Old Fish do lie
> 20 years he lived and then did die
> He was so tame you would understand
> He would come and eat out of your hand.
> Died April 20th 1855

From the mid-nineteenth century the craft of the monumental mason began to decline. The social upheaval of the industrial revolution saw the arrival of mass-produced memorials, and with them the invasion of 'foreign' stones and marbles. Classical designs were overtaken by Gothic and Greek revivals which were becoming familiar in English architecture of the time. Some were highly ornate, decorated with pinnacles and crockets, like the one among a collection of family memorials at Kingscote.

In any churchyard today there will be several almost identical headstones of the Gothic window shape as well as a few variations on the theme of the white marble cross, possibly draped with a foliage branch. In the churchyard above the river at Newnham-on-Severn is a crucifixion on a large plinth, standing in all about ten feet high and unique in this area.

In our own century little has changed, unless it is the lack of character that afflicts many of our modern cemeteries. Before there was some degree of control over churchyard memorials some oddities crept in, one of which is an erection in the churchyard at Idbury. It looks more like a landing craft on the moon than a graveyard

**Plate 35**. *Scalloped Bale tomb, Windrush*

**Plate 36**. *Farmer Perrott, Upper Cam*

**Plate 37**. *Marble and stone, Winchcombe*

memorial: it consists of a Celtic cross on flying buttresses and was built in 1907 in memory of Sir Benjamin Baker KCB KCMG FRS, king of the steel age, and his family.

Under a yew tree at Minsterworth is a white marble cross which is the modest memorial of F. W. Harvey, soldier-poet and 'Laureate' of Gloucestershire. He died on 13th February 1957 and a line on his headstone describes him simply as 'A Gloucestershire Lad.'

# Sculpture

From the simple rustic work in the Forest of Dean to the affluence of the Cotswolds there is a variety of skill, symbolism and humour which is a lasting memorial, literally, to the craft of the stonemason over hundreds of years.

The carvings of the sculptors of the late seventeenth and early eighteenth century are a natural progression from the corbel heads and grotesques that originated in pagan times and still decorate our Norman churches, inside and out. Early sculpture is best seen in the Forest of Dean, where it is well preserved in Forest stone: round-faced winged cherubs with foliage and books; at Littledean and Ruardean there are winged heads which look a little old to be cherubs; they are surrounded by round flower heads which have the simple charm of a child's drawing.

By the second half of the eighteenth century a certain sophistication had appeared which is well illustrated by a stone at Lydney dated 1743: two angels in strange headdresses blowing trumpets, with a lighted torch, representing immortality, on a stand between them. Their top halves are naked, showing them to be visibly female, their bottom halves disappearing into a cone like mermaids. Another one nearby has the same mermaid effect, one holding a book, tastefully covered in flowers and leaves with more heads peeping out between circles of cloud. The book represents faith and knowledge, with the Bible as the supreme Book. It appears constantly, often tucked beneath the chin of an angel with the fingers over the top.

The best examples of symbolic decoration are to be found on the magnificent chest tombs of Elmore, Standish, Haresfield and Painswick, where the four sides of a chest tomb or podium

**Plate 38**. *Trumpets and torch, Lydney*

gave more room for the full expression of the sculptor's skill. Here the symbols of mortality and death, skulls, skeletons, are balanced by the symbols of time and eternity: Father Time with his hourglass and scythe and that favourite representation of eternity, a serpent with its head in its mouth.

The Resurrection was another popular theme. At Dumbleton there are two unusually large stones to Richard Clayton and his wife Hester (1792) showing detailed pictures of the Resurrection on circular plaques surrounded by trailing foliage and urns. The dove appears in nearly every churchyard from the last quarter of the eighteenth century, often with a sprig of foliage in its beak, indicating the Holy Spirit and Peace.

Occasionally the sculptor's imagination seems to have run away with him: on a headstone dated 1801 at Withington is a damsel whose dress has fallen away, leaving the top half of her body naked. Opposite her is a cherub with an expression of acute embarrassment on his face and between them a dove flying out of the clouds, presumably to keep the peace.

Then there are stones which fall into no conventional pattern, but where the sculptor has developed his own imagery. On a headstone at Twyning dated 1852 the Hand of God is pointing down from the clouds to a draped ribbon.

The clouds are seen end on like Swiss rolls and behind them the rays of the sun form the background.

The variety and interest to be found in our churchyard memorials can really only be appreciated by walking among them. Many of our larger churchyards have gravestones in all shapes and forms covering nearly four hundred years. Malmesbury, Tetbury, Burford, Fairford, Chipping Campden all have exceptional collections; they offer a unique opportunity to appreciate the skills of craftsmen of a bygone age, rich in humour and symbolism.

**Plate 39**. *Tree of life, Littledean*

**Plate 40**. *Hand of God, Twyning*

**Plate 41**. *Angel with trumpet, Lydney*

# Materials

It is part of the attraction of country churchyards that the materials of the tombstones blend into the surroundings; that they should be part of the church, the buildings and boundaries, a sympathetic combination of colour, texture and design. Through them it is possible to identify the characteristics of individual local stonemasons with all the skill and originality of their work.

When the earliest churchyard memorials were made the only materials available to the craftsmen were those which were obtainable locally, usually stone from local quarries, and wood. Wooden graveboards can still be found in some parts of the country but I do not know of any in Gloucestershire and the Cotswolds. Here the vast majority of the original work was done in stone, which was not only plentiful but readily available, as almost every village had a quarry nearby. The names of the great stonemasons of the Georgian era are still remembered: the Strong family who owned the quarries at Little Barrington and Taynton; Joseph and John Bryan

of Painswick, father and son, of whom John lies buried under a plain pyramid in Painswick churchyard..

Cotswold limestone is soft on quarrying, and hardens with exposure. It does not weather well in comparison with slate, for instance, and on the great majority of the older headstones in our churchyards the inscriptions have worn away, features have been blunted by the elements, especially on the exposed south and west sides. Nor does it lend itself to the fine incised lines and detailed calligraphy of slate, but for deep carving it is unique. Because of its rough surface it is attractive to lichens and mosses, an enhancement by nature which is rarely found on polished marbles and granites.

The letter-cutters of the Cotswolds got round the problems of stone weathering by engraving inscriptions on to brass plates which were then fixed to the stone. This gave them a more receptive medium for their art, and a more lasting memorial for later generations to enjoy. They are to be seen all over the Cotswolds, many of them in highly decorative designs and often with amusing or poignant epitaphs.

The Forest sandstone is greyer than the Cotswold limestone and wears better; the details of seventeenth century carvings and inscriptions

**Plate 42**. *Dove of Peace, Twyning*

are still in good condition, and there is not a brass plate to be seen. Unfortunately Forest stone is subject to pollution and is now too expensive for modern sculptors.

Throughout the area there is a scattering of cast iron memorials; at Beverston there is a group of cast iron crosses to a local family of blacksmiths - as well as a handsome stone chest tomb to a blacksmith carved with a stone vase of flowers and foliage. In the Forest there are cast iron memorials in several churchyards, perhaps a relic of the iron-mining industry, with an odd one on a heavy base at Newland 'In memory of a devout and honest man John Weir Walkinshaw' who died in 1863 aged 77 years. At Lydney there is a cast iron plate on a ledger, and at Winchcombe a very decorative wrought iron cross is a memorial to the manager of Winchcombe gasworks who died in 1886.

There is a slate table tomb looking somewhat out of place at Berkeley, and a number of places have slate inserts on a stone background. There is a nice one at Lechlade, and at Minchinhampton and Cirencester there are several; obviously a local mason had hit upon this as an answer to the weathering problem.

**Plate 43**. *Ceramic hearts, Twyning*

**Plate 44**. *Cast iron memorial, Newnham*

With the development of the railways and canals other materials became available and one has only to look in any cemetery to see rows of mass-produced headstones in alien materials. When these creep into village churchyards it is a pity: at Idbury there is a polished heart in grey granite as well as a white marble headstone five feet high.

There are two other materials worth a mention: the memorial to Warren Hastings at Daylesford on the Oxfordshire border is in Coade Stone, an early nineteenth century artificial stone which is actually fired clay produced in London. The effect is slightly pinkish, the detail on the podium and urn still looking as good as when it was erected 150 years ago.

But the black mark for inappropriate materials must go to Twyning, in the north of the county. Here there are two pale yellow glazed ceramic hearts propped up on artificial logs - an excrescence in an otherwise interesting churchyard.

As well as Cotswold stone the modern sculptor has a number of English stones to choose

from, all with different properties and none of them offensive. A number of these are almost local to the Cotswolds: Blue Hornton from Banbury, a blue-green ferruginous mudstone which oxidises to a rust-colour. Severn Blue Lias, which can be polished to look like a marble comes from the same area; and Chicksgrove, from Tisbury, near Salisbury. From further afield there is Portland stone from Dorset; Purbeck 'Thornback', a buff-coloured stone also from Dorset and York stone which is similar in texture to Forest stone, and good for detailed work.

Fortunately there is still some excellent work being produced by recent generations of sculptors and letter-cutters. They show how good lettering and design can produce a memorial that is imaginative and aesthetically pleasing, which fits sympathetically into its setting and is what any monument should be, a fitting memorial to the deceased.

# Lettering

In the same way that the style of memorials changed over the centuries, so the art of the letter-cutter developed from the rough-cut inscriptions of the early 17th century to the flowery and decorative styles at the peak of the craftsman's art. It is not always possible to classify the different styles into specific periods; the spread of new ideas was affected by local geography and customs, by the types of stone available and by the skill of the stonemason himself and whether he was influenced by new trends in design.

The earliest inscribed headstones are from the beginning of the seventeenth century, about the same time that carved lettering first appeared on buildings. Some of the earlier masons were probably general craftsmen; their inscriptions have a primitive charm almost like the first efforts of a small child. The letters are crudely cut in Roman capitals; often the words are contracted - the word THE would often have only two uprights - and where they have run out of space the word is either written into the margin or carried over into the next line. It is common to find that where they were short of space small letters have been put in above the original ones, often seen in the word 'ye'. There is one at Woolstone that reads:

HEARE WAS BU
RYED THE ROBURT WEB
UPON THE 10 DAY
OF JULY ANN
HIS WIFE WAS
BURIED UPON
THE ? DAY OF
AUGUST 1657

From the beginning of the 18th century letter-cutting skills developed rapidly, largely due to the growth in printing and typesetting. As writing with a pen became a desirable skill for the children of the wealthy, writing masters produced 'copy-books' which were engraved on copper plates for printing, the origin of what became known as copper-plate handwriting. There is a good collection of inscribed stones covering a period of a hundred years at Aldsworth. Four of them from the 1770's have chubby cherubs, all for some reason looking to the left. On many stones in this area, and especially in the Forest of Dean where they are well preserved in Forest stone, the inscriptions are written in lower case, often decorated with curls and squiggles on the long strokes.

The 'Adam' styles popularised by the Adam brothers towards the end of the eighteenth century had a widespread influence in all areas of architecture. On churchyard memorials there was a movement towards urns and draperies, carefully swathed figures and floral sprays. Gradually the spread of 'pattern-books' with illustrations of lettering styles replaced the writing manuals, giving craftsmen the opportunity to expand their skills with new designs; by the beginning of the nineteenth century highly decorative styles were becoming fashionable, with flowing characters and embellished capitals surrounded by whorls and flourishes. In the Cotswolds there are some excellent examples on brass plates, some of them with the actual strokes of the letters also decorated.

By the middle of the nineteenth century fashion turned again to the plainer, heavier forms, although they were now available in a far greater range of designs and lettering. It became fashion-

**Plate 45**. *Primitive lettering, Woolstone*

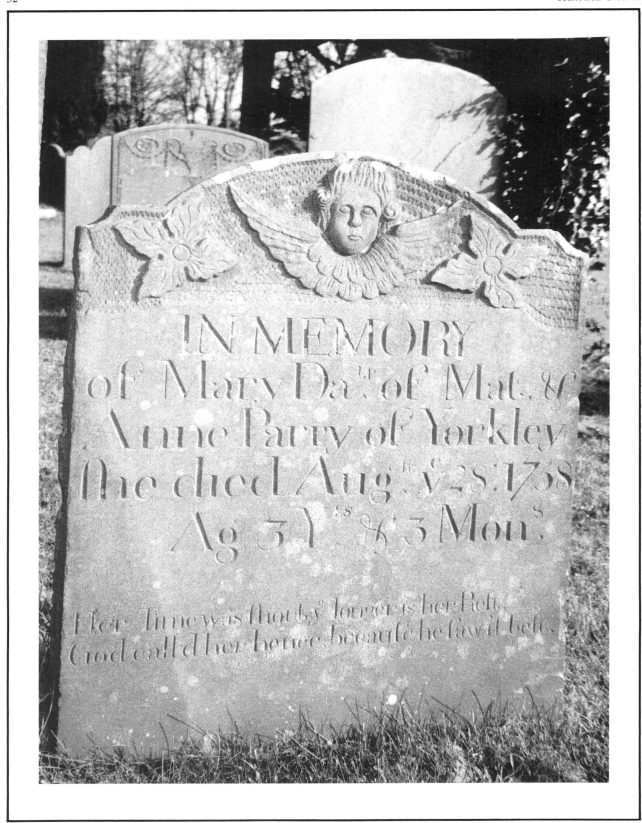

**Plate 46**. *18th century lettering, Lydney*

able to write the word 'sacred' or 'memory' in decorative or Gothic style with the rest of the inscription in plainer, less fluent lettering. Frequently several styles of lettering can be found on one stone, as though the stonemason was demonstrating the variety of his skills. There is a striking group of stones at Oddington with the artist's name cut into the stone; they were carved by Chambers of Stow. There are also good nineteenth century stones at Woolstone, Withington and many more.

Towards the end of the nineteenth century the art of the letter cutter began to decline as mass produced gravestones from the 'trade' began to fill the cemeteries, many of them in unsuitable marbles which neither mellow with nature nor weather with time.

# Brass plates.

The engraved brass plates which are a particular feature of the Cotswolds were a result of the poor weathering qualities of the Cotswold limestone, and they present an art form all of their own. The largest collection is at Painswick, but there are excellent ones to be seen in almost every Cotswold churchyard, notably at Minchinhampton, Kings Stanley, Miserden, Syde, Cirencester, Duntisbourne Abbotts and Sapperton, where the relatively recent brass to Ernest Gimson demonstrates the charm and simplicity of later forms of the art. He lies in the same churchyard as the Barnsley brothers, with whom he worked to create the Arts and Crafts tradition in the Cotswolds.

The earliest plate I have found is at Duntisbourne Rouse, a real cry from the heart:

An Elegie of Elizabeth Jefferis Wydowe of John Jefferis of Dunsburne upon his death who deceased the XII day of September 1611.

> Two bodyes one united hart conteind
> Fast linckt in loyall league of true affection
> But death that such a sweet content disdaind
> Mad of one halfe to immanure discretion

**Plate 47**. *Early 19th century lettering, Windrush*

> One halfe yet lives alasse why lives it longer
> It lives to make my greife and sorrowes stronger
> Yet till the time my fatall thred bee spannd
> My halfe shall pay perpetuall obsequies
> As fresh as when my firme love first begunne
> And deck thy hearse with endlesse elegies
> When in self same hearse desired shrine
> My body shall the last rest take by thine.

> We had VIII children
> IIII sonnes and IIII daughters as followeth
> John          Elizabeth
> George        Anne
> Thomas        Susana
> John          Elizabeth

This John Jefferis deceased was the youngest son, his father Richard Jefferis of Dunsburne.

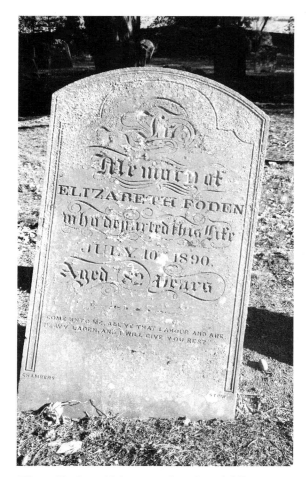

**Plate 48.** *Late 19th century lettering, Oddington*

There are also early plates at Burford, Hawling and Kingscote. The practice, which we would find strange, of giving the names of dead children to subsequent babies, is common on earlier plates.

At the southern end of the Cotswolds there seems to have been a particular appreciation of musical talent. A brass plate at Coaley marks the tomb of Mary Smith, a former organist, who died in 1796 aged 46. The plate shows a church organ complete with pipes, with underneath it the musical notation from Handel's Messiah and the words from the Book of Job, 'I know that my Redeemer liveth'.

There is a similar one at Uley to Thomas Ashmead who died in 1811 without the organ but with the music and words of 'All people that on earth do dwell.' And at Leonard Stanley a plate still in excellent condition is dedicated to:

Richard Henry youngest son of Samuel and Ann Holloway.
He was an excellent treble solo singer and highly respected for his uprightness through life. He died January 20th 1861 aged 50.

Also at Uley is a beautiful decorated brass plate to 'Roger Rutter alias Rudder who was buried August 30th 1771 having never eaten flesh, fish nor fowl during the course of his long life.' He died at the age of 84. According to 'Notes and Queries' he ate plain dump, whatever that may be. When tired of it he changed to hard dump and when in a 'special state of exhilaration' he added apple dump to his diet.

By the late eighteenth century brass plates had evolved into highly decorative forms, some so ornate as to be practically illegible. Many of them are signed, with a large number of the Painswick ones being ascribed to an engraver called Cook.

An inscription whether in stone, wood, metal or slate should have a visual appeal of its own, regardless of the message conveyed. This is certainly true of some of the modern work being produced by the sculptors and letter-cutters of today. Men like Bryant Fedden, Simon Verity and Rory Young are producing work of skill and originality which is keeping the art very much alive. Examples of their work can be seen at Winson, Hawkesbury Upton and Fairford, among others. Nor have our modern sculptors forgotten the importance of nature in our churchyards: the memorial to Nancy Mitford at Swinbrook has a relief carving of a mole, and a stone owl marks the grave of the furniture designer, Gordon Russell, at Chipping Campden. In the small churchyard at Owlpen, near Uley, a bronze bee decorates the stone designed by Bryant Fedden for Michael Lewis.

An organisation called *Memorials by Artists* keeps a register of many of the best letter cutters and memorial artists in the country. The object is for people looking for a well designed memorial to be put in contact with a suitable artist.

On an autumn evening we went to find the recent memorial by Simon Verity to the Duke and Duchess of Beaufort at Badminton. It's an estate church in the back garden of the big house, with the little churchyard no bigger than a tennis court and old headstones set into the wall. The tomb is so splendid it defies description: a lion rampant and a tubby dragon with fearsome eyebrows support the family coat of arms, the motto draped between them; above a moulded

**Plate 49.** *Modern headstone, Winson*

edge a stone crown sits on a tasselled stone cushion.

As we stood there waiting for the sun to come out of the trees a dog fox sauntered by. He stood and watched us for a few moments before hopping over the wall and away. It was the first day of the Beaufort Hunt, we later heard. I hope he was the one that got away.

# Preservation or Decay?

A walk round almost any of our churchyards will demonstrate the problems that face incumbents and Parochial Church Councils. Tilting, sinking headstones and crumbling chest tombs bear witness to the ravages of time and weather. The cost of repairing them all would be prohibitive and understandably many feel that the limited resources available should be spent on the fabric and maintenance of the church itself.

Crumbling tombs are a danger as well as an eyesore, and the numbers in need of repair may be in the hundreds. A tomb that looks fairly solid may have been in a precarious state for years. In many cases the stone may be in good condition and in need only of simple structural repair, the cost of which may not be any more than the cost of demolition and having the vault made safe. The Diocesan Advisory Committee can supply a list of contractors with experience of this type of work.

Where the condition of the stone has deteriorated to such an extent that it can't be saved it will either have to be removed or extensive repairs carried out. Stone decay is unpredictable; one side of a chest tomb may be crumbling while the rest of it, stone taken from the same quarry at the same time, is in good condition. This is because stone beds differ even in the same quarry.

The cost of restoration or stone conservation like that which has been carried out at Painswick and Harescombe is another matter. The detailed specialist work is delicate and time-consuming, and therefore expensive. It is debatable how many of even our most intricate tombs merit this sort of attention, or whether they should be left to nature, to gather lichens on the blunted features of their cherubs and to weather gently over the passage of time.

A great number of our churchyard memorials are listed, some of them as Grade II★, meaning that they are of special interest and cannot be demolished or altered without permission. Details of listings are held by the District Council, the Record Office and English Heritage.

The Diocesan Advisory Committee acts as Trustee to the Table Tombs Fund, set up by the late Dame Joan Evans in 1960 as a reflection of her concern for these beautiful and irreplaceable monuments. They are able to make small grants towards repairs, and tombs of exceptional value may be eligible for a conservation grant from the Council for the Care of Churches.

What memorials we may or may not erect in our churchyards is controlled by the diocese, who see themselves as having a responsibility to preserve their beauty and maintain some control over the introduction of inappropriate designs or

**Plate 50**. *Headstone with bee, Owlpen*

**Plate 51**. *Memorial to the Duke and Duchess of Beaufort, Badminton*

# GRAVE MEMORIAL RECORDING FORM

| | CEMETERY or GRAVEYARD | COMPTON ABDALE, GLOS. | | | | | | | |
|---|---|---|---|---|---|---|---|---|---|
| | DEDICATION or DENOMINATION | ST. OSWALD.    C. OF E. | | | | | | | |
| 1 | NAT. GRID REF. | | | | | S | P | 0 5 9 1 6 6 |
| 2 | DATE of RECORD | | | | | | | 1 | 0 0 6 8 4 |
| 3 | NAME of RECORDER or GROUP | COMPTON ABDALE W.I. | | | | | | | |
| 4 | MEMORIAL No. and LETTER | | | | | | | | 0 0 0 4 3 |
| 5 | No. of COMPONENTS | | | | | | | | 0 1 |
| 6 | ASSOCIATED FORM LETTERS | | | | | | | | |
| 7 | Memorial type: 1. flat  2. head  3. tomb  4. foot  5. other | | | | | | | | 3 |
| 8 | MATERIAL and GEOLOGY | LIMESTONE | | | | | | | |
| 9 | STONE MASON or UNDERTAKER | | | | | | | | |
| 10 | Which faces are inscribed? — compass points | | | | | | | | 0 0 7 3 |
| 11 | No. of people commemorated | | | | | | | | ? |
| 12 | TECHNIQUE of INSCRIPTION | CARVED | | | | | | | |
| 13 | Condition of monument: 1. sound, in situ    2. sound displaced   3 leaning or falling apart    4. collapsed    5. overgrown | | | | | | | | 3 |
| 14 | Condition of inscription: 1. mint  2. clear but worn   3. mainly decipherable  4. traces  5. illegible or destroyed | | | | | | | | 5 |
| 15 | DIMENSIONS (in mms.) | Height | | | | | | | 0 4 8 5 |
| 16 | | Width | | | | | | | 0 6 1 0 |
| 17 | | ~~Thickness~~ LENGTH | | | | | | | 1 8 3 0 |
| 18 | PHOTOGRAPH NEGATIVE No. | | | | | | | | |
| 19 | ORIENTATION | [compass diagram] which way stone faces | | | | | | | 3 |

| PHOTOGRAPH | INSCRIPTION |
|---|---|
| 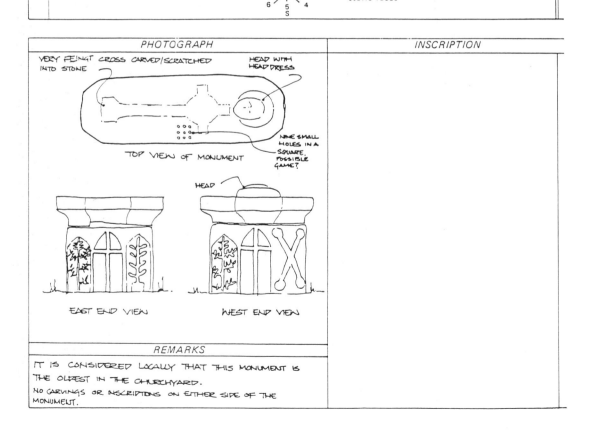 VERY FEINGT CROSS CARVED/SCRATCHED INTO STONE — HEAD WITH HEAD DRESS — NINE SMALL HOLES IN A SQUARE, POSSIBLE GAME? — TOP VIEW OF MONUMENT — HEAD — EAST END VIEW — WEST END VIEW | |

### REMARKS

IT IS CONSIDERED LOCALLY THAT THIS MONUMENT IS THE OLDEST IN THE CHURCHYARD.
NO CARVINGS OR INSCRIPTIONS ON EITHER SIDE OF THE MONUMENT.

**Figure 2**. *Grave memorial Recording Form used for W.I Surveys.*

materials. For instance granite or marble is not encouraged, and anyone wishing to erect a memorial in either of these will have to get permission (known as a faculty) from the Diocesan Advisory Committee. However they do encourage imaginative individual designs and hand-cut lettering in local stone or one of a similar appearance.

It is worth noting that there is no automatic right to erect a memorial in a churchyard. Strictly speaking, every memorial requires a faculty, although in practice the incumbent is

authorised to grant permission within certain limits. The maximum size of headstone allowed within the Gloucester Diocese is :

| Height | 4'0" (1200mm) |
|---|---|
| Width | 3'0" ( 900mm) |
| Thickness | 6" ( 150mm) |

All other types of memorial, such as ledgers, crosses and kerbstones require a faculty.

Since 1953 'unseemly' epitaphs have been banned, and inscriptions have become largely factual with perhaps only a line from the Bible in addition to the name and date.

In the early 1980's a number of Women's Institutes carried out churchyard surveys in their own villages. These now provide a fascinating record of hundreds of individual monuments, in some cases with illustrations.

**Plate 52**. *Crumbling tombs, Bourton-on-the-Water*

**Plate 53**. *Restored chest tomb, Painswick*

In a separate survey carried out in the large churchyard at Newland two women recorded 1,000 memorials, leaving their small children inside the railings of a chest tomb as an improvised playpen while they undertook the survey.

Where churches have been taken over by the Redundant Churches Fund - the Eastleaches, Lassington, Ozleworth - the churchyards surrounding them are not necessarily in their care. They try to make arrangements with local naturalists trusts or individuals, but otherwise they cut conventionally, perhaps three times a year. At Lassington this treatment pays off; the churchyard is full of daffodils and cowslips in the spring, while invasive brambles and nettles are kept under control.

# Epitaphs

The study of epitaphs provides a fascinating insight into the lives of our ancestors. They are a reflection of contemporary life with all its frailties and tragedies; of whole families, tiny children, faithful servants. Of what they did; how they lived and often how they died.

The inscriptions on the earliest memorials were simply factual, with only the name of the deceased and when he died, presumably because the stones were small and lettering skills fairly limited. One of the earliest epitaphs is on the chest tomb at Hardwicke to Hannah daughter of William Smith who died in 1695. The inscription with its reminder of mortality is still legible almost three hundred years later:

> Although my body lyes in Dust
> My soul in Christ did ever Trust
> Weep not for me least you offend
> But seek your lives for to amend
> And while thou readest this of me
> Think on the Glass that runs for Thee

The craft reached its peak during the eighteenth century as letter-cutting skills developed. The epitaphs, especially in the Forest of Dean were often simple with a moral tone like this one at Awre to Anny wife of Philip Smith who died in 1741:

> Look on me and learn to die
> You must be dust as well as I

Or this concise one from Duntisbourne Abbotts:

> Young ones may, old ones must
> Quickly die and turn to dust.

In the Cotswolds where the craft of engraving on brass plates was developing rapidly they were becoming increasingly sentimental and flowery. This one from Sapperton is a good example:

> Rebekah wife of Cha Mason Jun. with the greatest serenity of mind she departed this life on 17th February 1759 at Greenwich, Kent in the 21st year of her life.
>   Could the unsully'd art from
>     Dissolution save
>   In vain might Death assum'd this silent
>     grave
>   But Fate how hard!
>   Her sable morn in dark shades expire
>   And noontide Sun went down with
>     Job's desire.

In the same churchyard is an epitaph that is a sad reflection on family strife to: Mary daughter of Wm and Jane Gardner who died 31st May 1792 aged 44.

> Her husband void of humanity to perpetuate her memory, her SON in respectful remembrance caus'd this TABLET to be erected over her sleeping dust.

In the days when there was no effective relief from pain and illness, epitaphs similar to this one from Elmore are to be found in nearly every churchyard:

**Plate 54**. *Brass plate, Westonbirt*

Affliction sore long time I bore
All human help was vain
Till God did please Death should me seize
And ease me of my pain.

Remembering the high death rate from diseases which have now been eradicated, this one from Minchinhampton is also very common:

The pale consumption struck the fatal blow
The stroke was severe but the effect came slow
With wasting pains Christ saw me sore oppress'd
Pity'd my soul and kindly gave me rest.

# Children

Infant mortality was very high and it was not uncommon for six or seven children to have died in the same family, often with the same names being given to subsequent children. Epitaphs to children were often flowery, like this one at Minchinhampton to a child aged six:

Death Nip'd this little lovely CHILD of
ours
As the hoary FROST nips tender flowers
So all our CARE and GRIEF was spent in
vain
Though parted NOW we hope through
CHRIST to meet again.

Death in childbirth was also common. A headstone at Lassington reads simply:

Hester wife of Thomas Moye who deceased in childbirth August 17th 1693 as also her little one with her.

An epitaph written in dialect is a rarity indeed; sadly the well-recorded one at Dymock seems to have disappeared, perhaps a victim of recent building works:

Too sweeter babes youm nare did see
Than God amity give to Wee
But they were ortaken wee ague fits
And yur they Lies as dead as Nits

There is a most attractive headstone at Newland to two small children both with the same name:

Joseph Rosser died September ye 10th 1711 aged 1 year 6 months also Joseph died Sep 23 1714 aged (sic) 2yrs.

Though death our tender reeds have
shaken
Yet Christ ye pretty babes have taken
Weep not for us from tears refrain
We hope in Heav'n to meet again.

And another sad little one at Brimpsfield to Susanah, daughter of John and Mary Fewings who died April 5th 1831 aged 2 years 6 months:

> Her Cup of life just with her lips she prest
> Found the taste bitter and refused the rest
> Averse then turning from the face of day
> She softly sigh'd her little soul away

In the churchyard at Woolstone is a more recent stone to Norman Thomas who was accidently killed on December 24th 1956. It reads simply:

> A good little boy.

What a terrible Christmas present for his family.

## Accidental death

Drowning was a common cause of death before the arrival of the railways gave families access to the seaside. The churchyards along the Severn are full of headstones to children who have drowned in the river. The most graphic of these is the headstone by the gate at Newnham which shows in great detail a scene on the 'Bristol river' with a rowing boat tipped up and two youths falling out of it, a sailing vessel and a paddle steamer complete with crew. The epitaph reads:

Sacred to the memory of David Merrett aged 24 yrs and Samuel Jones aged 17 years both of Newnham who were drowned in the Bristol River August 29th 1848

> Beneath this spot two youths most justly dear
> In the same tomb were laid with many a tear
> Alas recovered from a watery bed
> Only to slumber here mid dust instead
> Four youthful friends that fated boat contained
> But two alone in life the shore regained
> O heed young man this truth and feel the power
> Death oft and quickly crops the fairest flower

**Plate 55.** *18th century headstone with epitaph, Lydney*

> No present health or circumstance can save
> From what may be thy doom, an early grave
> Art thou rejoicing in the bloom of youth?
> Seek Him who is the Way, the Life, the Truth
> And ere for thee be turned the churchyard sod
> Prepare in heart and soul to meet thy God.

It was not only children who were drowned. A brass plate at Barnsley records the death of Thomas Norris who died in 1816 aged 35:

> O! Death, how sudden was thy stroke,
> The nearest Union thou has broke,
> Nor gave me time to take my leave,
> Of my dear Parents left to grieve;
> The watery waves which stop'd my breath,
> For want of help soon caused my death.

In the churchyard at Dymock is a splendid tapered chest tomb to the two young Hooper lads who drowned in the River Leadon on November 30th 1824 aged 28 and 18:

**Plate 56**. *Brass plate to singer, Leonard Stanley*

In perfect health we went from home
Not thinking that our Glass was run
The running flood of water strong
It did our Bodies overcome
For God above who thought it fit
To lay our body in the Deep
Now parents dear forbear to mourn
We wait the resurrection morn.

Another epitaph at Duntisbourne Abbotts to a young man called William Beames carries a salutary message. He died in 1799 at the age of 22.

A warning peice (sic) to all young men
Who in their blooming age
Misspend their time and know not when
They must go off the stage.

Unexpected death is also reflected in this memorial at Brimpsfield to William Bird, Yeoman of Caudle Green, who died on February 20th 1794 aged 58:

I went forth well, and passing on the way
Death sore surprised me and made me stay
Strangers and pilgrims in the world we are
O think on me thou fellow traveller.

Or this more recent one at Twyning to Ada Louise Halling who died in 1934 aged 45:

We little thought when you left home
You would no more return
That you so soon in death would sleep
And leave us both to mourn.
Could I have raised your dying head
Or heard your last farewell
The blow would not have been so hard
For us who loved you well.

And we may never know what happened to Isaac Ballinger of Cheltenham, who died in 1721.

Reader! Pray covet not this world,
Out of it you may soon be hurled,
For as a wheel it turns about
And it was a wheel that turned me out.

Perhaps the most unusual epitaph is the one at Malmesbury to Hannah Twynnoy who died on October 23rd 1703 after being attacked by a tiger that had escaped from a travelling circus:

In bloom of Life
She's snatch'd from hence
She had not room
To make defence;
For Tyger fierce
Took Life away,
And here she lies
In a bed of Clay
Until the Resurrection Day

# Murder

There are several epitaphs to people who met there death by foul play like this one from Awre to:

Joseph ye son of William and Eleanor Mathews. Who was Murder'd March ye 26 1783 aged 36 years.

Be thou my rock to whom I may
Thy promise is to help alway
Save me my God from wicked men
From folk unjust and also them.

Or this one from Sapperton:

William Fowler, miller and baker, who was supposed to be robbed and murder'd by some person or persons unknown as he was returning from Cirencester market which place he had frequented more than 40 years. This melancholy accident happened February 20 1792 in the sixty fourth year of his life.

Sudden change ah quickly we beset
I had not time to bid my friends farewell
But all must die where place or when is
    known
To God but not to man.

And finally a very odd epitaph from English Bicknor to William Cooper who died in 1729:

I grive to think that I can grive no more
For thou my loving friend.

# Trades and Professions

It was common practice for the occupation of the deceased to be recorded on their tombstones, and some are a reflection of the industries prevalent in the areas. In the Cotswolds there are clothiers everywhere, while the Forest has a predominance of master mariners, ships' captains and Severn pilots. On the exterior north wall of Stroud church is a unique collection of small brass plates which make up a remarkable record of the trades in the town over two hundred years. Here there are clothiers of course, but also butchers and bakers, a confectioner and a farrier, a soldier and a Justice of the Peace, a stay-maker and a peruke-maker.

Set in the paving of the churchyard is a superb engraved plate to a man who evidently died from the effects of inoculation:

> Here lie the remains of Richard Merrett, watch and clockmaker who died under inoculation December 17 1767 aged 67 years.
> He was an ingenious mechanic sincere friend and Christian true to the faith of this Redeemer. It was his request therefore let no sacrilegious hand disturb his ashes but permit them to rest in this gloomy mansion till the last trumpet shall awaken him to Life and Immortality.

> Let those who to these awful Cells repair
> To waste an hour or ease the soul of care.
> Stop one short moment near his plaintive stone
> And with the tears of friendship mix their own.
> Then take the last advice by Merrett given
> Be virtuous now, leave all the rest to Heaven.

The most famous epitaph to a watchmaker is the one at Berkeley to Thomas Pierce:

> Here lyeth Thomas Pierce, whom no man taught
> Yet he in Iron Brasse and Silver wrought.
> He Jacks, and Clocks, and Watches (with Art) made

> And mended too when others work did fade
> Of Berkeley five times Mayor this Artist was
> And yet this Mayor, this Artist was but grasse
> When his owne Watch was downe on the last Day
> He that made Watches had not made a Key
> To Winde it Up, but Useless it must lie
> Untill he Rise Again no more to die.

In the same churchyard is a plain chest tomb to a jester who was buried on June 18th 1728 at the age of 63:

> Men call'd him Dicky Pearce
> His folly serv'd to make folks laugh
> When wit and mirth were scarce.
> Poor Dick alas! is dead and gone
> What signifies to cry?
> Dickys enough are still behind
> To laugh at by and by.

Ralph Bigland says that this epitaph was written by Dean Swift, Chaplain to Charles, Earl of Berkeley, whose own epitaph was also written by Swift.

At Upleadon, north-west of Gloucester is a blacksmith's tomb which bears the epitaph:

> In memory of James Broadstock Blacksmith, who died Jany 31st 1768 aged near 50 years.

> My sledge and hammer he's reclined
> My bellows too has lost his wind
> My fire extinct my forge decayed
> And in the dust my vice is laid
> My coal is burnt my Iron's gone
> My nails is drove thy work is done.

There is an identical one, dated 1796, in the churchyard of St Mary, Cheltenham.

Another allegorical one is carved on a stone at Newnham to Thomas Yerbury who died in 1759 at the age of 67. Presumably he was a seafaring man, but the use of capitals lends emphasis to his domestic strife:

> From ev'ry blustrous Storm of Life
> And that worse Storm Domestic Strife
> Which shipwrecks all our social Joys
> And ev'ry worldly Bliss destroys
> I luck'ly am arrived at last
> And safe in port my anchors cast
> Where sheltered by the blissful shore
> Nought shall disturb or vex me more

Here Lyeth Thomas peirce, whom no man taught
Yet he in Iron Brasse and Silver wrought
He Jacks, and Clocks, and watches (with Art) made
And mended too when others worke did fade
of Berkeley fiue tymes Major this Artist was
And yet this Major, this Artist was but Grasse
When his owne watch was Downe on the last Day
He that made watches, had not made A Key
To winde it Vp, but Vselesse it must lie,
Vntill he Rise AGaine no more to die.

But joys serene and calmest peace
Which Christ bestows shall never cease.

**Plate 57.** *Memorial to Thomas Pierce, Berkeley*

The various occupations listed on tombstones are too numerous to mention, but some of the more unusual ones are: Forest Keeper (Littledean); Collector of Taxes (Minchinhampton); Ironmaster (Newnham); Page to George IV (Blockley); Victualler (Kings Stanley); Gardener (Elkstone) Wheelwright (Winchcombe). A brass plate on the porch wall at Duntisbourne Abbotts reads:

Parish ClerkBe neath this place lieth Anthony Sly of this Parish. He died the 9th day of July 1736 aged 93 years.

Servants were well appreciated and a number of churchyards have epitaphs to servants like this one at Twyning to John Harris who died on the 2nd April 1807 aged 49:

In steady fidelity and attachment for the family which he served during a period of seven and twenty years. In patience under frequent bodily pain and resignation to the seemingly severe dispensations of Providence proved faith in Christ have any claims to respect from man and to humble though well grounded hope of mercy from a Creator it may be truly said that the deceased were justly founded.

Perhaps the strangest epitaph is the one also at Cheltenham to William Higgs who died in 1825:

Here lies John Higgs
A famous man for killing pigs,
For killing pigs was his delight
Both morning, afternoon and night.
Both heats and cold he did endure
Which no physician could e'er cure.
His knife is laid, his work is done
I hope to heaven his soul is gone.

Or the one that relates the sad end of Ann Collins, a barmaid of Kings Stanley who died on 1804 aged 49:

Twas as she tript from cask to cask
In at a bung hole quickly fell
Suffocation was her task
She had not time to say farewell.

The last word must go to the nineteenth century lines that are found in several churchyards. This one is at Burford and is dated 1849:

Praises on stones are titles vainly spent
A man's good name is his best monument

# Nature in our Churchyards

In recent years the value of our churchyards for the conservation of wildlife has been increasingly recognised. Natural grassland and lowland hay meadows have all but disappeared under mechanised farming with its chemicals and fertilizers. But our churchyards, carved out of ancient pastures, unploughed and unsprayed, remain a refuge not only for ourselves but also for all forms of wildlife, including some of our threatened species. A churchyard of less than an acre may contain over a hundred different flowering plants and ferns.

Among the mellow stones there will be birds, butterflies and moths, insects, lichens, small mammals, perhaps even frogs and toads, slowworms and glow-worms. Others may be just passing through: the fox we saw at Longney was as surprised to see us as we were to see him, and there may also be bats, badgers, rabbits, stoats and weasels. Together they make up a living landscape, a hive of activity showing that the churchyard is a sanctuary very much for the living as well as the dead.

At one time neglected and overgrown rural churchyards would rapidly have been re-colonised from the surrounding agricultural land, but the majority of our fields are now so barren that accidental colonisation can no longer be left to chance.

**Figure 3**. *Wildlife in the churchyard (The Living Churchyard)*

In his foreword to Francesca Greenoak's beautiful book, God's Acre, Richard Mabey writes:

'At present, churchyards are regarded principally as resting places for the dead, where a respectful, sombre tidiness, clipped of the excesses of nature, ought to prevail. That is an understandable feeling, but in the light of our growing sense of the interdependence of all life, a more hospitable attitude towards the rest of natural creation might perhaps be an apter Christian response.'

## Churchyard Habitats

The wildlife found in one churchyard will never be the same as in another, even in the neighbouring parish because the habitats depend on variable factors: the type of soil, the drainage, the aspect and degree of protection from the elements and the amount of management previously carried out.

The church itself can easily be overlooked as a supporter of wildlife; lichens and mosses will colonise the outside walls; from vantage points on tower or spire sharp-eyed owls and kestrels

Swift

Kestrel

Bats

House Martins and Swallow nests

Swallow

Barn Owl

Rabbits

House Martin

Owl Pellet

Mole Hills

Ox-eye Daisy

Harebell

Lichens

Pepper Saxifrage

Quaking Grass

Bulbous Buttercup

Leaf

Field Scabious

Flower

Vole

Yellow Rattle

Meadow Saxifrage

Mouse

Sulphur Clover

Bird's foot Trefoil

Common Spotted Orchid

Shrew

Mouse-ear Hawkweed

Fruits

Cowslip

keep a lookout in the longer grass for their next meal; some of them may even be nesting in the belfry. House martins, swifts and sparrows will build their nests in the nooks and crannies of the outside walls, and bats may roost and hibernate, not, as popular belief would have it, in the belfry, but in the roof.

Boundary walls are important sites for lichens, mosses and ferns, and dry stone walling is a favourite habitat for a small snail called *balea perversa*. Another small white subterranean snail which is blind has a liking for the cavities of bones, and is widely found in limestone areas.

A number of churchyard trees will provide nesting sites for birds: rooks, tawny owls, woodpeckers and nuthatches. Trees native to Britain such as oak, ash, maple, holly, hazel or rowan, also provide winter food for birds and small mammals. Yews are favourite nesting sites for the greenfinch, chaffinch, mistlethrush and coal tit. Lime trees, often lining the paths, are very attractive to bees. Dead trees are also valuable as nesting and roosting sites for birds and bats, while rotting wood will be home to insects and fungi and a larder for woodpeckers. In spring and summer, churchyards like Dymock and Hewelsfield are alive with birdsong — blackbirds, robins, wrens, tree-creepers, woodpeckers, nuthatches and many more.

All churchyards have an area of grassland. It may consist of different grass species as well as wild flowers. Where mowing is less frequent and flowers have been able to set seed there may be lady's smock and cowslips in the spring, poppies and cow parsley in summer. In the spring daffodils will push their heads through the grass; snowdrops and bluebells will spread under hedges and overhanging trees. At the Eastleaches and at Dymock people come from miles to see the daffodils in spring. Native flowering shrubs are a source of nectar for butterflies, bees and other insects, and later in the year birds will be attracted to the fruit and seeds. Some species, like slow-worms, like medium-length grass, but for the glow-worms at Woolaston, what is the point in glowing if the grass is too long for you to be seen?

There is a piece of folklore in Gloucestershire which says that spring is not here until you can cover twelve daisies with one foot. Daisies are about all that will survive close mowing, which makes a churchyard look more like a garden than an area of natural beauty. At the other end of the scale grass that is never cut will have an accumulated mass of dead vegetation underneath which wild flowers cannot penetrate and which only insects and a few small mammals will appreciate. Ultimately brambles and small saplings will

appear as the land begins its natural regression to woodland.

Hedges and boundaries with native shrubs and bushes provide nectar for insects, and berries, seeds and nesting sites for birds. Primroses and cuckoo pint will grow at their feet, and an A-shaped hedge will provide cover for small mammals. In a survey on birds' breeding sites in churchyards carried out for the British Trust for Ornithology it was found that the blackbird was the species most commonly present, followed by the greenfinch and the robin and a dozen others of our common species, including the wren, chaffinch, linnet and mistle-thrush. In the churchyard at Idbury there is a birdbath memorial on the boundary wall, and on the day we were there in early autumn grey squirrels were bounding through the grass.

Finally, in some hidden corner of the churchyard there will be a compost heap, with last year's mowings warm and welcoming to insects, hedgehogs, perhaps even slow-worms and toads. A larder and a builders' merchant for birds, rich in food and nesting materials.

## Bats

For many people bats have sinister associations. They are creatures of the night, but they do not suck blood or get tangled in your hair. They are small furry creatures and they are a protected species. They are found in areas where there is a good supply of insects for food: trees and ponds and the flora of old meadowlands. There are a number of colonies in buildings along the Severn.

Greater Horseshoe bats and Long-eared bats like the high roof spaces of churches, but their droppings fall on to the pews and the altar, making them unpopular with clergymen and cleaners alike.

Pipistrelles are crevice dwellers, favouring the space between the tiles and the felt. At Woolaston in the Forest of Dean there is a breeding colony in the roof of the church and David Priddis, Batman of the Forest, once hand-reared an abandoned baby for a month. Unfortunately it died, but a great deal was learnt from the experience.

At Westbury, Greater Horseshoe bats, so called because of the horseshoe shape of the nose, use both porches as night time feeding roosts in small groups, returning to the breeding colony by day. Understandably bats do not appreciate churches being illuminated at night, and it is enough to drive them away, although the Horseshoe bats at Gloucester Cathedral seemed to avoid the floodlighting; instead they were setting off the alarms.

In the church at Winchcombe the lady doing the flowers told me how she had found a bat in an empty vase. Thinking it was probably dead she put it carefully in the fork of a tree and from there it flew away.

## Butterflies

Butterflies like churchyards too, especially the Holly Blue for whom the holly and the ivy are its main sources of food, and which lays its eggs on the unopened flower buds of each alternately. Other varieties such as the Common Meadow Brown and more rarely the Marbled White need the flora of longer grass for breeding, and will be eradicated if the grass is mown too early in the year. The Speckled Wood prefers the shaded areas of the churchyard where the grass is shaded by tall trees, while the Wall Brown favours full sun, and likes the tall grasses left along a wall or tombstone. The Gatekeeper is a hedgerow butterfly, and may be seen round the perimeter of a churchyard. The butterflies that normally frequent gardens, such as the Tortoiseshell, Red Admiral and Painted Lady appreciate a small patch of nettles for their larvae to feed on; they can be encouraged by the usual butterfly plants like buddleia.

## Invertebrates

A churchyard that has not been over-managed will be home to several species of invertebrates, who favour an untidy corner with old stones and miscellaneous rockwork. An uncommon woodlouse, *porcellionides pruinosus* is found in the churchyard at Coberley, near Cheltenham. It has dispersed into the surrounding habitat from the dung and straw in the stables of Coberley Court.

Spiders live in the crevices of stonework, in the bark of mature trees and in bushes and grassland. The Common Brown 'Wolf' spiders are active in sunshine and can be seen running over paths and gravel areas, while the Common Garden spider, who builds a large orb-web, can be found everywhere where bushes and scrub occur.

The Meadow Grasshopper is found widely in Gloucestershire where the grass is longer and ungrazed, while the Common Field Grasshopper likes grass that is mown short or grazed. Also common among brambles and scrub is the vocal Dark Bush Cricket. Its cousin the Speckled Bush Cricket is well-camouflaged and almost inaudible, and is more difficult to find.

## Lichens

Anyone who is a regular visitor to churchyards will have noticed the yellow and white blotches that decorate the surfaces of gravestones, walls and trees. Lichens are a particular type of fungus which lives in association with an alga. The algae produce food from carbon dioxide and water by photosynthesis, and the nutrients are absorbed by the fungus.

Lichens take a long time to become established and are very slow-growing, gaining as little as 0.6mm in a year. They do not like to be dis-

turbed, which is why they are found on ancient buildings such as churches, and on tombstones. A church will offer a number of varied habitats: different varieties will grow on the different aspects of the building: the flora of the cool north side will not be the same as the sun-loving species on the south side. Window mullions and lintels, different mortars used over the years, will all have a different chemical composition and will attract a wide variety of species.

In the churchyard the gravestones, especially the older ones, will be made of several types of stone; their surfaces will have weathered differently, depending on aspect, exposure and protection from trees. On one tomb the incised carvings and inscriptions may attract different species

from the smooth stone. Where bird droppings have enriched the top surface of a headstone the conditions will again be conducive to other varieties.

Because the chemical composition of limestone provides a favourable habitat for lichens there is a wide variety of species in Gloucestershire and the Cotswolds. In the churchyard at Burford is a rosette of a yellow lichen called *Caloplaca aurantia* on a tomb dated 1756. Assuming it colonised the stone soon after erection, it has grown 135mm (from centre to periphery) in 236 years, a growth rate of 0.57mm per year. A total of 71 species have been identified at Burford, many of them of particular interest. This compares with between 84 and 150 found in the 'top twenty' lichen-rich churchyards in the country.

At Westwell 58 species have been recorded and at Fulbrook and Taynton 52 and 47 respectively. Churchyard trees which have been established for many years also provide a habitat for lichens, although conifers and yews, which have very acid bark, are not hospitable sites. Paths and

lawns can also be colonised as can materials apart from stone, such as metal and wood. It is common in the Cotswolds to find an area of runoff where brass plates have oxidised, and here the chemistry of the stone will have altered drastically, providing a new habitat for the species.

# Yew Trees

Yew trees are held in such affection by churchyard enthusiasts that they are worthy of a special mention. Traditionally longbows, effective weapon of Plantagenet kings, were made from yew, although doubt has been cast on this theory recently. Threatened by the advance of the Black Prince who was flushed with victory after the battles at Crecy and Agincourt, the Spanish stopped the export of yews to England. Because they were poisonous to cattle, farmers refused to grow them, so they were planted in churchyards. When gunpowder came into use under the Tudors the demand for the longbow ceased, but by then yews were well established in churchyards and many of them are still standing.

Allen Meredith knows more about yew trees than anyone: he has an affinity with them that is almost telepathic. For the last few years he has lived, slept and dreamed yew trees. In his work with the Yew Tree Campaign he has dated and recorded over 400 trees in gardens, churchyards and ancient sites, many of them several thousand years old. He is hoping to establish official recognition for the protection of the most ancient of these trees.

Allen can establish the approximate age of a tree from a number of factors. Ring counting is impossible, because older trees can put down new roots and renew themselves from inside out. In his estimations for ageing yew trees Allen asks for the following information:

1. Location and grid reference of tree if possible
2. Name of church, if any, and position of tree in relation to church
3. Details of ancient burial mounds, barrows or other archaeological site within 200 metres of the tree.
4. Legends, local folk stories or historical facts relating to the tree.

5. Records of the tree, including measurements made in the past.
6. Girth of tree at three feet and four feet above ground level.
7. Is the tree hollow?
8. Is the tree male or female? ie. Are there berries in early winter?
9. Photograph please, if possible.

Girth measurements can be used as a rule of thumb, although growth can slow down or even stop for centuries while the tree remains active and alive. Allen has produced the following table as a guide to the age of yew trees:

| GIRTH | AGE IN YEARS |
|---|---|
| 9 ft | 242 |
| 11 ft | 292 |
| 18 ft | 720 |
| 19 ft 8 ins | 820 |
| 24 ft 5.5 ins | 1360 |
| 27 ft 2 ins | 1810 |
| 30 ft | 2400 |
| 33 ft | 3000 |
| 35 ft | 4400 |
| 35 ft 6 ins | 5000 |
| 36 ft | 5600 |

From these figures it can be calculated that there are several very ancient trees in Gloucestershire and the Cotswolds. Among those with the largest girth are:

| | |
|---|---|
| Awre | 22 ft |
| Broadwell | 23 ft |
| Huntley | 21 ft |
| Hewelsfield | 21 ft |
| Lydney | 20 ft |
| Pauntley | 24 ft |
| Staunton (Glos) | 31 ft. |

Many churches now have certificates from the Conservation Foundation, verifying the age of their tree and perhaps affording it the respect and recognition it deserves.

# Management for Conservation

Managing a churchyard for conservation can in itself be a cause of conflict. Those who would like to see it mown as smooth as a bowling green imagine that conservation means neglect, that long grass and nettles will be allowed to take over. In fact conservation is a compromise which may reduce the amount of work, with sympathetic management of different areas providing differing habitats. If it is neglected altogether scrub and brambles will rapidly take over.

The most efficient way to embark on a new plan of management is to make a survey; in that way the wildlife already taking advantage of the habitats will not be disturbed and the needs of people using the churchyard will be respected. Where graves are still being tended they must be accessible and areas that are in use, such as those where cremation plaques are placed, the grass should be kept short.

# Grassland

The aim should be to provide a balance, with areas of grass of different lengths providing a variety of habitats. In general the approach to the church and areas where access is needed, for instance to the compost heap, will be mown close. The cuttings should be raked off so that new growth is not smothered Areas of longer grass where spring flowers grow should not be cut until July, by which time the plants will have flowered and set seed and the new generations of butterflies will have flown. It can then be cut again in October to leave it ready for the next spring.

Summer flowering meadow should be cut in the spring between April and June, then left through the summer and cut again in late autumn. The mowings should be raked off after every cutting, or the decaying grass will encourage the growth of rank grass at the expense of flowers.

Obviously most parts of the churchyard will have flowers that span the whole season and it will be necessary to identify which ones are important and plan accordingly. Many of the traditional churchyard and meadow flowers such as cowslips, harebells, can be raised from seed. Small areas should be left totally uncut, perhaps along the boundary, to provide cover for small mammals, lizards, and slow worms.

In mediaeval times churchyards were largely kept under control by grazing, and it was a joy recently to find sheep in part of the churchyard at North Cerney. Goats like churchyards too, but have to be tethered or they will consume everything in sight.

## Walls and Hedges

Walls are valuable habitats, especially for mosses, ferns and lichens and should on no account should be sprayed or cleaned. Hedges be trimmed only in January and February to avoid disturbing nesting birds. They should preferably be cut to an A-shape, thick at the base and narrow at the top, so that rain and snow run off without damage and cover is provided for small mammals and nesting birds.

Ivy can damage gravestones and walls when its aerial roots eat into the stonework. Ivy on tombs should be cut out at the base and only removed when it has died off. Ivy does not kill trees other than yew, and it is important that some should be left, as it is an important nesting site for birds and is home to a number of insects.

## Introducing new plants

Native plants which are introduced to the churchyard should be selected for their attraction to wildlife. Trees and shrubs such as hazel, holly, hawthorn, crab apple and buddleia. Wild flower seeds can be bought from specialist seedsmen or seeds gathered from the wild. These are best germinated in trays and planted out as seedlings.

In view of the increase in recent years in the number of cremations, some Parochial Church Councils have set aside a designated area, sometimes called a 'Garden of Remembrance' for cremation plaques. This has been done at Hardwicke, where a secluded part of the churchyard has been surrounded with shrubs to provide a quiet corner for rest and reflection.

## Information

The 'Living Churchyards' campaign was launched in May 1989 to promote the practice of sympathetic churchyard management for wildlife. It is supported by the Church and Conservation Project, Community Service Volunteers and the Royal Society for Nature Conservation. The 'Living Churchyard' Information Pack gives advice on carrying out surveys, preparing management plans, and where to get additional help. The pack is available from any of the organisations mentioned; audio/video cassettes can be obtained from the Church and Conservation Project. For the past two years churchyard management training days have been arranged for church representatives together with naturalists and conservationists. Also in the pack are details of churchyard competitions which reflect the current interest in conservation, and information on grants..

In the Gloucester Diocese there is an annual competition for the best-kept churchyard, one in each Archdeaconry of Gloucester and Cheltenham. The criteria are improvement and maintenance, concentrating on the human contribution, with regrettably no emphasis on conservation.

The Gloucestershire Trust for Nature Conservation recognises the importance of churchyards for wildlife. The Trust will give advice on request on how such areas should be managed for the benefit of the wild plants and animals which find refuge in churchyards. The Trust is happy to support any scheme which promotes churchyard conservation.

# Selected Churchyards

## Bisley

The village lies to the north of Stroud, above the mills of the Golden Valley, and was once the centre of a large parish which included Stroud. Weavers cottages are scattered like pebbles down the hillside, the jumble of gabled roofs reflecting all the colours of local stone. Surrounding houses bear testimony to the wealth of successful clothiers and wool-merchants.

All Saints' churchyard has probably been a sacred site since pagan times; during restoration work in the nineteenth century two Roman altars were found built into the wall of the church and fragments of Anglo-Saxon stonework were also unearthed.

Below the churchyard is Seven Springs, a well where seven spouts of water pour into a semi-circular basin, once used to wash the yarns of the wool trade. Sacred rites were performed here in pagan times, and since 1863 a well-dressing ceremony has taken place every year on Ascension Day.

Ralph Bigland thought the name was derived from bees: 'In Domesday Book an annual rent is specified, as due to the Manor, of Two Quarts of Honey. This Circumstance is singular and seems to confirm the Idea that this Parish derived its Name from Bees, so many of them being here cultivated, as to render their Produce of Consequence to the Demesne.'

The churchyard is full of brass plates to clothiers and merchants, many of them on heavy ledger stones and beautifully inscribed. Some of them died young, like the one from 1792 to a clothier who was only twenty three. It seems to express some doubt about the hereafter:

> Stand reader here a little time
> Consider here lies one
> Was taken off just in his prime
> To Heaven I hope he's gone.

The treasure in this churchyard is a thirteenth century well head which is thought to be the only outside one of its kind. It is a six-sided stone structure with trefoiled arches and on top a stubby spire and cross, the whole thing only about twelve feet high. It was probably built as a combined churchyard lantern, or poor souls'

**Plate 58**. *Poor souls' light, Bisley*

**Plate 59**. *Railed tomb, Bisley*

light, and a cross. The wealthy would donate
candles for the souls of the poor, hoping perhaps
that in due course their own souls would benefit
from their charity. It covers a well and is known
locally as the 'Bonehouse'. There is a legend that
on a dark night a priest who was summoned to a
sick parishioner never arrived. His body was later
found down the well, which was then covered
over so that it could never happen again. As a
result Bisley was excommunicated for two years
and all burials were carried out at Bibury.

There is one memorial in the churchyard
which is a rare depiction, possibly a portrait,
although it is very worn. It shows the top half of
a female figure with her arms folded in front of
her and smaller full length cherubs on either
side. Kenneth Lindley dates it as late seventeenth
or early eighteenth century but thinks it is
unlikely to be a portrait.

There are other epitaphs, many of them typical of the period. One from 1807 bears a reference to the Grim Reaper:

> While he in painful sickness lay
> Grim Death did hurry him away
> From his loving wife and children dear
> For to lie here till Christ appear.

# Elkstone

The church of St. John, Elkstone, famous for its
Norman work, is the highest church in the
Cotswolds, and from here one would expect
panoramic views in summer and roaring gales in
winter. But the perimeter of the churchyard is
surrounded by trees and the church stands in
peaceful Norman dignity, as though unmoved by
the advance of the twentieth century. The
churchyard is tidy but not over-mown; there is
lady's smock and bluebells among the tombstones, the edges left long for the smaller inhabitants under the trees.

In this churchyard there is a feeling that you
are not alone. Grotesque gargoyles with large
heads and squat bodies lean out from the battlemented parapet of the tower, leering with open
mouths at passers-by. Lower down are two
figures playing musical instruments, a shawm
and a citole, with a grotesque animal on either
shoulder. The carvings are crisp, the work perhaps of a mediaeval mason with a sense of
humour when the tower was rebuilt in the
fifteenth century.

But that is not all. The carvings continue on
the north and south side on a well-preserved corbel table. Here there is an odd collection of creatures: a centaur, a griffin, a devil, a ram and

**Plate 60**. *Knowles chest tomb, Elkstone*

many more animals and birds. No wonder there is a feeling of being watched.

Looking at the east wall from outside, the small east window has a surround of battlemented sunk-fret ornament which is probably unique. Above it is a plain window which used to provide access for the birds to the columbarium, or dovecote, above, now only accessible from an interior spiral staircase.

Over the thirteenth century porch is an apexstone on the gable which is hollow, and may once have been for an All Souls Light. Inside the porch and protected by it from the elements is a carved tympanum which is one of the most exceptional pieces of Norman work in the country. It depicts the figure of Christ in Majesty on a cushioned throne, holding the Books of Judgement in his left hand and giving the blessing with his right, while above on the left is the Lamb of God. Around Him are the winged symbols of the four Evangelists, and pointing down is the Hand of God. The beakhead ornament surrounding this is in excellent condition, the carvings easily identifiable as a serpent and a lion, and an inverted figure grasping the snouts of its neighbours.

In the churchyard there are two fine seventeenth century Renaissance table tombs to the Poole family with two girls sitting comfortably on skulls surrounded by elegant draperies. Each skull has thoughtfully been raised on a stand to give it the right height — an excellent demonstration of the skill and humour of the stonemason and comparable only with those of Elmore, Standish and Painswick.

There is a good ledger stone with a typical moralistic epitaph of the mid-nineteenth century:

In memory of George Ebsworth of this village, Yeoman who died October 5th 1844 aged 74 years:
> Farewel vain world we've had our day
> We care not now what thou of us mayst say
> Thy praise we heed not nor thy censure fear
> For all that mortal was lies senseless here
> What fault thou'st seen in us take care to shun
> Look well at home there's something to be done.

Unique to this churchyard is a pair of recent headstones in seventeenth century traditional style with copperplate lettering, dated 1936 and 1950. They give a very good idea of what the

**Plate 61.** *Scroll end chest tomb, Elkstone*

many old and worn headstones of that period would have looked like when they were first cut.

In the corner of the churchyard, its lower windows at grass level, is a building which was a priest's house from the fourteenth to seventeenth century. Like the grotesques and the corbelheads, it is watching over this churchyard, where perhaps the stonemasons who carved the figures with such wit and exuberance lie among the unmarked graves of centuries ago.

# Elmore

Elmore lies on the banks of the Severn, where in spring the narrowing river bank causes the Severn Bore to wash over the wellies of the unwary. It is only a hamlet, a scattering of small cottages and timbered houses along a pretty winding road, but its churchyard contains what is undoubtably one of the finest chest tombs in the country.

It is a memorial to Arthur Knowles, who died in 1707, and carries rich symbolic carving in high relief. The skill in the execution of this tomb, like those of Haresfield and Standish, makes it hard to believe that this was the work of a local mason

in a remote Severnside hamlet. Frederick Burgess in English Churchyard Memorials describes it as 'allegorical figures in contemporary costume clinging to the Scriptures for salvation, flanked by the grim personages of Time with his customary scythe and hourglass standing on a wheel, and Death as a cadaver holding his dart trampling a globe.'

The only way to appreciate this carving is to go and look at it. On the south face the figures curve round the central cartouche, from which the inscription is now lost, with plump angels blowing trumpets straight into their ears. Beneath them little figures with curly hair sit on foreshortened skulls, a highly accomplished piece of carving. All the spaces on the panel are filled and the details of the faces, the clothes, even the fingers are well preserved.

On the north side the inscription is still legible, beautifully written on a circular cartouche. A gentleman in a curled wig and a long coat is resting his foot nonchalantly on a skull, while opposite him a female figure with a rounded face is wearing a loose robe, her foot also on a skull. Unfortunately the top half of the skeleton is missing. The lyre ends are also richly carved with acanthus leaves and heraldic panels.

There are pedestal tombs with cherub heads and gadrooned balusters on the corners; coronets and skulls, books and serpents. In the corner stand the ruins of the Guise family mausoleum. It is described by Bigland as it was in its former glory: 'an arcade of four arches finished with a pyramid of freestone, erected over the vault of the Family of Guise.' It is thought to be the earliest use of the Roman order, and it is sad to see it in disrepair.

The epitaphs at Elmore are rewarding; some of them well preserved in Forest stone. One by the south porch reads:

> Here lyeth the body of Daniell ye (sic)Sonn of Daniell Ellis who Departed this Life ye 14th of Decem (sic) 1672.
>
>> Though in my Prime surprised was by Death
>> Who did bereave me of my Life and Breath
>> But yet the tirant (sic) he could not controle
>> That my Redeemer dear died for my soul.

And another one to the same family who seemed delighted at the prospect of death. It is written in unusual Gothic script:

> Here resteth the body of Daniel Ellis Snr who deceased ye life the 6th day of August Anno Dom 1664 and also Elizabeth his wife who

**Plate 62.** *Cherubs, Elmore*

died the 31st Mar Anno Dom 1686.
>In life we lived in grave conjoined we lye
>Waiting an happy Immortality
>(sic)Wee soared aloft on Souls ascended
>    high
>With wings of Faith did to Heaven fly.

There are twin headstones dated 1746 with
usual relief carving executed in great detail.
ie fond epitaph on one of them reads:

>Farewell dear wife must we now part
>That lay so near each others heart
>The time will come I hope when we
>Will both enjoy Felicitie.

# airford

e church of St Mary, famous for its medieval
ss, has a great deal that is worth looking at
m the churchyard. It was built by John Tame,
ich wool merchant, in the high Perpendicular
le, with solid parapets and crocketed pinnacles
ng two levels. There are carved figures every-
ere; along the string courses are grotesque ani-
ls from ancient bestiaries, a ram, a lamb and a
vern. On the southern string course is a figure
own as the climbing boy, a jester in a large

headdress dangling a leg over the edge as though
about to jump.

On the clock face of the tower there is the
Warwick gryphon in bold relief, and below it a
huge carving of a man's head, with one hand
holding a scourge. On the parapet is carved the
Warwick arms and badge, a muzzled bear climbing a ragged staff. Here too are local tools of the
tradesmen, blacksmith's tongs, a hunter's horn,
horseshoes, while on the north face are a dragon
and a wine vat.

The west side has a figure of Christ of Pity
with His right hand raised in blessing and in his
left hand the Resurrection Cross. Above are the
armorial bearings of John Tame, the rich wool
merchant who rebuilt the church towards the
end of the 15th century, a wyvern fighting a lion,
with on one side the shears and gloves of the
wool trade, and on the other the shell of a salt-
trader.

At each corner of the tower are dumpy
grotesque figures with hats and swords, each
with a padlock over their heads, one apparently
needing three keys to open it.

The tombs in the churchyard are a mixed
bunch, with something of everything. The
upright headstones of the seventeenth century
show weathered angels and cherubs, circles of
foliage which would once have contained the
inscription. There are some good examples of
mid-nineteenth century lettering on upright
stones, well incised and still legible. In the newer
section to the north of the churchyard is a good
modern headstone to Michael John Peachey.

By the south door is a very old Gothic tomb
with quatrefoils; much too old to have an inscription, but unusually wide, either for a person of
unusual breadth, or like a double bed, for two.
Close to it is a tomb with a coffin-shaped slab on
top, complete with carved stone handles at the
ends. On the end is a worn carving which looks
more like a child's head than a cherub, with her
fingers over the top of a book.

There is a good bale tomb to the stonemason
and quarryman Valentine Strong with the initials
V S 1662 and carvings of foliage and flowers on
the side panels. In the scalloped end of the bale
is a handsome winged skull, in good condition.
There are several plain pedestal tombs, one from
1823 to a gentleman whose surname was Harvey
which has carved on the four corners full length
figures in long gowns, their hair in ancient-Egyp-
tian style. Had he travelled to Egypt in those
dangerous times? Was he an authority, a writer
perhaps?

Under the east wall there are two almost identical pedestal tombs, one dated 1797. They are
decorated with all the possible emblems of time
and eternity: books, an hourglass, a hand mirror,

a trumpet and an hourglass. The inscriptions are almost gone, but the carvings on the ends show round-cheeked cherubs modestly draped.

Opposite the church door under the eye of a statue of the Virgin and Child over the porch, is a small white headstone with a carving of a cat. It is the memorial to Tiddles, the church cat, 1963 — 1980.

On the old school wall overlooking the churchyard is a plaque to:

> Mr Richard Green, late Master of this Free-school who departed this Life the 9th day of November 1767 in the fifty fourth year of his Age.

**Plate 63**. *Climbing boy, Fairford*

The Integrity of his Life and Manners had gained him the sincere Respect of his Neighbours, and the uncommon Assiduity and Abilities with which he discharged the Duties of his Profession for more than fourteen Years in this School, have made his Death a Publick Loss, and he will be long lamented by all those that know the Value of so useful a Character.

# Haresfield

Haresfield is difficult to find; the driveway is unobtrusive, and is shared with the Manor, so that one walks self-consciously in front of the windows of the house. The tip is off the spire and there are gargoyles on the tower. Otherwise the church is plain, apart from the clock, once a sundial, dated 1692.

The churchyard is wide and level, with a pleasing wrought iron fence separating it from meadows and mature trees. The chest tombs are a reflection, again, of the astonishing skills of local craftsmen, with deep carvings and rich symbolic figures.

On the north side there is a group of older chest tombs, distinguishable by the narrower body and greater overhang, the inscriptions in Roman lettering still legible in parts. Nearby is another group of five plain tombs, many sharing the same name with archaic spelling:

> HEARE RESTETH THE BODY OF JHONE LONGE, THE WIFE OF ROGER LONGE DECESSID THE EIGHTEENTH DAIE OF DECEMBER 168 ..

And in the same group:

> HEARE RESTETH THE BODY OF WILLIAM WARNER, CLOTHIER, WHO DECEASED THE 20 DAY OF SEPTEMBER AN.DOM.1632 WAITING FOR A JOYFULL RESURRECTION

On the same side of the church are some excellent carved tombs with weepers in long gowns, heads resting on hands, eyes demurely closed. Alongside them are flowers and fruit, curling leaves of foliage, ribbons and drapes.

The Niblett family has a number of tombs here, including an unusual chest tomb dated 1816 and decorated with quatrefoils and battlements like a miniature castle, perhaps a copy of a mediaeval style.

**Plate 64**. *Carved lyre ends, Haresfield*

The south side has several deep-carved chest tombs of a slightly later date. Two, side by side, have their lyre-ends carved with angels, one with her hands holding a book, the other over a cartouche, with all fingers and thumbs clearly visible.

Three chest tombs to the Niblett family which are protected by a yew tree are perhaps the best preserved we have seen. They are only six inches apart, so that the inside surfaces are in excellent condition and still legible. One is to Judith the wife of Daniel Nibblett, yeoman, who departed this life the 16th day of Jan Anno Dom 1694 *aetatis fuae* 32. Beautiful individual figures with hair in a roll and chubby thighs are holding back the curtains from an oval frame.

On another are big-faced round cherubs, their hair parted in the middle with a style that looks almost modern. The lyre ends are intricately carved with a bewigged figure like the ones at Standish, hearts, flowers and leaves. Next to the three is a later podium also to the Niblett family carved with three cherubs, which is an interesting example of the complete change of style a hundred years later.

Another lyre-ended tomb is a memorial with skulls and draperies to Samuel Birt who died the 25th February 1712/13 (written as a fraction) aged 58 years. On one side is a little cherub, its head on its hand, the other hand resting on a skull. On the opposite side is another one with a well preserved face, holding open a book with its thumb, its other hand resting on a tool of some sort. On a neighbouring tomb, obviously the work of the same man, are all the symbols of death and eternity: a bearded Father Time holding an hourglass, a full length skeleton, winged cherubs.

A number of brass plates are signed by Hamlett, including one to Thomas Warder who died October 17th 1830:

> A friend so true there were but few
> And difficult to find
> A Man more just and true to trust
> There is not left behind.

# Hewelsfield

You come to Hewelsfield (Hiwoldestone in the Domesday Book) through steep narrow lanes, past grey farm barns and sheep-dotted fields. Behind you the view improves as you climb: the silver streak of the river, the hamlets of the Vale and beyond, the wooded slopes of the Cotswold scarp.

The church stands 600 ft up on the watershed between the Severn and the Wye. The circular churchyard indicates that this may have been the site of ancient pagan rituals, where sacrificial ceremonies were carried out to pacify the gods. This is battle-scarred border country, and two sections of Offa's dyke within the parish are reminders of its bloody history. The churchyard in its prime position for defence may well have been a circular ditch containing a fortified camp.

The churchyard is dominated by a great yew tree, certified by the Yew Tree Foundation to be 1300 years old. On the north side of the church the roof comes down to within a few feet of the ground, and with the stubby Norman tower gives the church a feel of being part of the earth on which it stands.

There are some nice Forest stones in the churchyard; faces and figures well preserved, including an odd carving of a figure lying on a couch looking most uncomfortable. On one stone there is a face with thick hair cut straight across the forehead. The inscription is to Hannah, daughter of Henry and Margaret Worgan, who died ye 20th November 1709 aged eleven years:

> My plant did flourish fair
> Like to a rose in June
> But Death with his cold blasting air
> Has cropt my tender bloom.

And on the same stone their son Nathaniel who drowned at the age of 21:

> Say not when you these lines explore
> The sailor falls to rise no more
> For when the Trump of God shall call
> He'll rise again no more to fall.

There seem to have been a number of drownings in the parish. John Darby died on the 8th

**Plate 65.** *Kingscote family memorials, Kingscote*

October 1798 aged 30 and one of his sons drowned with five others in 1825. The inscription reads:

> Awful and suddenly untimely death
> In flood of sorrow I resign'd my breath
> The flashing torrent was my dying bed
> No friend to close my eyes nor raise my head
> Ah! While affection heaves for me a sigh
> In order set thine house for thou must die.

Two members of the Bowen family drowned in separate incidents. Richard Bowen drowned in the River Wye in 1871 aged 31 years:

> In the cold stream my limbs were chilled
> My blood with deadly horror thrilled
> My feeble veins forgot to play
> I fainted, sank and died away.

This churchyard is exceptional for the care and detail with which the wildlife has been recorded. Inside the church is an illustrated list of thirty-five different flowers, assorted trees and grasses, and twenty different species of birds, including swallows which nest in the lych gate. There are also sixteen species of small mammals and insects, ending with:

> moles (numerous)
> goats (visiting with permission)
> cats (without permission)

The full lists and records of tombstones can also be seen in the W.I Surveys at Gloucestershire Record Office.

# Kingscote

Kingscote lies in a dip in the Cotswold plateau above Dursley. In spring the lane is bunched with snowdrops, the houses basking sleepily in the sun. In May the curved stone walls are splashed with aubretia, and the churchyard is mauve with a carpet of lady's smock.

Inside the gate is a stone sundial with a bulbous stalk on a square base. The inscription on it reads:

> This is the Lord's Garden, Sacred to Him, Sacred to them.
> Rest here.
> Eternal rest grant unto them Oh Lord and let light perpetual shine upon them.
> Let nothing defile it.
> Speak and act reverently.

On the church there are crockets on the tower which has a small spire in one corner. A simple plaque inside the porch reads:

Edward Jenner 1749 - 1823 was married in this church to Catherine Kingscote 6th March 1788. His work in connection with the introduction of vaccination has made him forever dear to the human race. His marriage brought him much happiness.

On the south side of the church is a chest tomb written in the haphazard lettering of the seventeenth century. The last line could have more than one interpretation:

> HERE LYETH THE BODY OF
> EDMOND BALL WHO DEPA
> RTED THIS LIFE THE ? DAY OF
> APRELL IN THE YEARS 1662
> HERE WAS A PAINFULL HUSBAND
> ...

There is also a tall chest tomb with the end carved with open books, an hourglass, a cross and a crown. Sadly this tomb has since collapsed.

In the corner of this churchyard is a unique collection of memorials to the Kingscote family, One of them, a well-preserved chest tomb, is thought to be the oldest known memorial to a soldier. It is a narrow tomb with a large overhang, an indication that it is an early tomb. The inscription in stone is still legible:

> Here lyeth the Body of Troylus Kingscote Gent
> Who did service as a Commander for the Prince of Orange
> 40 yeares and Being 80 yeares old ended
> This Life upon the tenth day of September Anno Dni 1656

A flat ledger records that his wife outlived him by a few years:

> HERE RESTETH THE
> BONES OF ALLIDAY, THE
> WIFE OF TROYLIUS
> KINGSCOTE, GENT WHO
> DEPARTED THIS LIFE
> THE 17 DAY OF AUGUST
> ANNO DOMINI 1662

On an early brass plate is a long epitaph to Anthony Kingscote Esqr, who 'fell asleepe in the lord on the 29th of August in the yeare of Christ 1654. The archaic language and spelling make it read oddly to us. He composed his own epitaph, which was uncommon:

> Mistery of Misteryes, thou art hee:
> Whose like was not nor ere shall bee:
> That Maiesty divine was ioyned in
> With loathsome darkness of sinn:
> That God of glory dayned to take
> Curse, death and torments for our sake.
> Hee did refuse the Angells state
> And Abrahams seed upon him take.
> To dye for enimyes and those
> Who were becomde his utter foes:
> To dye for us to make us good
> Who all in curst corruption stood
> To rayse us out of graves and hell
> With him in light and life to dwell
> Tremble with joy to think upon
> This most misterious union
> Glory to God mercy to man
> Is Heavens proclamation.
>     Anto. Kingscot
>     So thought
>     So wrote
> Which doth declare his faith and prove
> His part in Gods eternall love.

Nearby, and only three years later is a superb decorated brass plate to Anne, who must have been his daughter:

> HERE LYETH THE BODY OF
> ANNE KINGSCOTE, THE 4TH
> DAUGHTER OF ANTHONY AND
> KATHERINE KINGSCOTE, WHO
> ENDED THIS LIFE UPON THE 9TH
> DAY OF NOVEMBER, IN THE
> YEAR OF CHRIST 1657

His wife outlived them both, and lies under a flat stone, the inscription still legible under a layer of moss:

> KATHERINE, THE WIFE
> OF ANTHONY KINGSCOTE,
> ESQ DECEASED
> THE 2 DAY OF
> DECEMBER 1665

Later members are recorded on a fairly hideous Gothic memorial, inscriptions written in illegible letters of the same style and also a shield with the Kingscote family crest hanging from a stone strap. In the same corner is a Roman coffin dug up in an adjacent field.

Among the ledgers set into the ground is one which says:

> ENTRANCE TO VAULT

# Littledean

The churchyards of the Forest of Dean are a far cry from the intricately carved tombs and elegant brass plates of the Cotswolds. Littledean is a working town at the edge of the Forest, a winding street with cottages jostling for room on the pavement.

The outside of the church is unremarkable apart from two scratch dials on the south wall of the porch. and the interesting fact that the clock has two nines but no eleven. On the north side the churchyard has been cleared, except for one railed chest tomb in the centre. Among the headstones now propped around the edge is one to Samule Beard:

> Sacred to the memory Of Samule Beard
> Late a Police Sergeant at Littledean who was brutally beaten by four men at the Speech House when in the discharge of his duty on the night of the 17 August and died from the effects on 24 August 1861. Aged 37 years. Esteemed and Respected by the whole Force for his Integrity, Punctuality and Exemplary discharge of his duties.

The south side is fortunately undisturbed. Here is a unique collection of Forest stones with many highly original carvings characteristic of the area. A feast of flowers and foliage, of cherubs with bulging cheeks; of the symbols for time, eternity and immortality: a serpent biting its tail, a winged hourglass, a torch. On the headstone to John Reynolds, one of ye Keepers of the Forest of Dean who died in May 1740 aged 47, there is a carving which may be the man himself, surrounded by angel wings and flowers.

On a six-foot headstone is a half-relief figure of a child which is surely a portrait in stone. The inscription has entirely flaked away except for a small portion which has a fragment of 'Suffer the little children'. Who was he? What did he die of and when?

The greatest tragedy recorded in this churchyard is the death of four young men, the youngest only twelve, in a disaster at Bilston Pit.

> These four youths were suddenly called into eternity on Tuesday the 6th day of April 1819 by an awful dispensation of the Almighty. The link of a chain employed to lower them into Bilston Pit breaking they were precipitated to the bottom of the pit. Their bones literally dashed to pieces, their bodies thus presenting a frightful and appalling spectacle to all

**Plate 66**. *Headstone to a little boy, Littledean*

**Plate 67**. *Headstone to a Forest keeper, Littledean*

beheld them. They were interred in one grave on the Friday following being Good Friday April 9th 1819. A Funeral Sermon was preached on the mournful occa-sion on Sunday April 25th 1819 In the Church of Little Deane before a congregation of 2500 people on the following text which it was judged advisable to record upon their Tombstone as a suitable admonition for the benefit of all survivors.

Luke XIII vs 1, 2, & 3.

Swift flew the appointed messenger of death
and in a moment stopt their mortal breath.
Art THOU prepared as suddenly to die?
Tis mercy's call O list unto the cry.

    Thomas Morgan Aged 26
    William Tingle Aged 19
    Robert Tingle Aged 16
    James Meridith Aged 12

# Miserden

Miserden is one of those pleasant, undisturbed villages that is pure Cotswold: grey stone mul-

lioned cottages, aubretia spilling over walls, a church with a dumpy tower overlooking the green expanse of Misarden Park. Wild flowers grow among the gravestones; mature trees keep the elements at bay.

A pleasing small lychgate leads into the churchyard, with a magnificent yew arch, neatly trimmed, dominating the front of the church. The oldest chest tomb found so far is on the south side of the church. The inscription is protected by the overhang and is still legible after nearly three hundred and eighty years:

> HEARE WEARE BURIED THE BODYS
> OF
> ANTHONY OCKHOVLD AND TACEY
> HIS WIFE
> WHICH ANTHONY DECEASED THE
> 24 OF MAY 1605
> AND TACEY THE 15 OF JANUARY
> 1612

The name Tacey is also found elsewhere, for instance at Hewelsfield.

There is a good collection of inscriptions, including several occupations: two plumbers on the same slate slab, an innholder, a baker, a shepherd, and a plasterer who came to a sad end. He must have been desperate for work to leave his family:

> In Memory of William Ferne of this Parish (Plasterer) whose death was occasioned by a fall from a Building in London July 14th 1861 in the 44th year of his age, leaving a widow and six children.

The epitaph to a shepherd has a feel of his dedication to his work:

> Samuel Horrell native of this Place, but late of Tetbury in this County, a shepherd, who departed this life the 10th of April 1807 aged 54 years.

> From youth through life the sheep was all his care
> And harmless as the flock his manners were
> On earth he held the faith to Christians given
> In hope to join the fold of Christ in Heaven

There are a number of epitaphs that refer to neighbours, like this one:

> To the pious memory of Ann the wife of John Coates of this Parish, yeoman. She departed this life December 11th 1772 aged 39 years

**Plate 68**. *Yew tree arch, Miserden*

> A peacefull neighbour resteth here
> A loving wife and mother dear
> To help the poor she grudged not
> Can such a friend be soon forgot.

Also near this place lies Peter their son who died in his Infancy

This one is slightly odd. Are they neighbours to each other, and why is the death of the wife not recorded?

John Bradley April 26 1834 aged 50 years

> A loving father, mother dear
> Two peacefull Neighbours resteth here
> In hopes to Christ to raise from Dust
> And blessed be among the Just.

Perhaps the epitaphs were all composed by the same person, or was this a Gloucestershire oddity?

> To the memory of Daniel Gibbons Senior of this Parish and Sarah his wife. She departed this life the 15th October 1773 aged 70 years. He departed this life 27 November 1783 aged 81 years

> Beneath here lyes two peaceful neighbours dust
> Who in the Lord did always put their trust
> Just and sincere till by Death call'd away
> Hoping through Christ to rise to endless Joy.

There are modern tombstones here too: two memorials to the Sinclair family, one a ledger, the other a nicely-lettered slate on a short column. There is also a square slate with an attractive circular inscription which reads:

Remember John Alexander Harper 1917-1986 Priest of this parish 1971-1982. In the centre is written: Te Deum Laudamus

# Painswick

Mention a Cotswold churchyard and it is Painswick that comes to mind, described by Alec Clifton Taylor as the finest collection of Georgian tombs in the country.

The setting is perfect: the elegant spire beckons from the surrounding hills to a village of pure Cotswold; gracious buildings of mellow grey stone, gabled roofs, steep narrow streets where little cottages whisper together on the pavement.

The best way into the churchyard is through the lychgate, which was made partly from old timbers from the belfry with barge-boards carved with bells. It is part of a row of cottages and has stone seats and a little upstairs room.

Painswick is famous for its ninety nine yews which line the paths across the churchyard and are beautifully trimmed. They were planted about 1792 and legend has it that there are always ninety nine: that if a hundredth is planted one will die, although in fact there are many more.

The churchyard memorials are a reflection of the affluence of the great wool merchants and of the skill of local stonemasons. Here there are chest tombs carved with angels and cherubs, little boys tastefully draped to preserve their dignity, skeletons and bat winged skulls. There are pedestal and tea caddy tombs in all shapes and sizes and plain headstones, including one from 1783 to Thomas Hamlett, Senior Free Mason, whose signature is on many of the brass plates in the churchyard. It is carved with the arms of the Masons' Company flanked by masons' tools with an angel's head above and flowers and fruit round the edge. John Bryan who lived from 1716 to 1787 and was responsible for much of the superb craftsmanship in Painswick churchyard, is buried under a plain stone pyramid.

Recently some restoration work has been carried out on some of the tombs and the improvement is noticeable. On the tomb to Edward Palling, Clothier, 1758, the rococo cartouche and the lozenge patterned borders are in good condition, as is the single scroll supporting the ends, one with a bat-winged skull. There is an excellent Tomb Trail leaflet available in the church.

Painswick also has a good collection of brass plates, some with beautiful lettering. One of them must be the most long-winded in the Cotswolds. The plate is fixed to an upright Gothic podium and it reads:

To the memory of the late William Hogg who died at a very advanced age on the 8th November 1800. He was for 50 years a much esteemed gratuitous Preacher of the Gospel In the Tabernacles of London, Bristol, Rodborough and various other places in this and adjoining counties. It is incredible the sums of money he expended in charity. Also of Betty his excellent wife who died 31st March 1780. Her kindness and liberality especially to the poor was gratefully remembered and often expressed for many years after her decease. They had eight sons and four daughters whom they lived to see comfortably established in life.

It seems the inhabitants of Painswick were long-lived for their time. Henry Jordan died in November 10th 1801:

Ninety three years on earth I spent
And left my poor frail tenement
In Silent dust for to remain
Till rais'd by Christ to Life again.

Paul Mills died in 1795 aged only 38 years and his memorial reads:

When God cut short the thread of Life
Then fatal Death parts man and wife.
His wife lived another 50 years and died at
   the age of 82 in 1845

Richard Townsend who died in 1794 aged 45 seems to have no regrets:

Farewell vain world I've seen enough of
   thee
In grief and pain, sickness and miserye
Thy smile I value not nor frowns do fear

**Plate 69**. *Headstone to Thomas Hamlett, Senior Free Mason, Painswick*

Thanks be to God I sleep as quiet here
What fault you've seen in me still strive to shun
Look at home: there's something to be done.

Finally, there's poor Hannah Carter:

In the Well Looking Bloom of Her Life, She
Was suddenly Seized by Disease on the Morning of
April 17 1833
She did (sic) on the Evening of the Same Day.

In 'Gloucestershire Notes and Queries' is a copy of a newspaper report about William Cook whose death was announced on 25th February 1837 aged 89, 'who for nearly 70 years filled the situation of gravedigger in that parish. During that period he provided graves for nearly double the population of that Parish having dug, or caused to be dug, the extraordinary number of 6,267 graves and in that time he also provided graves for seven of the parish clerks.'

In September a ceremony takes place at Painswick called the Clipping Service. It is held on Feast Sunday, which is the Sunday on or after September 19th. It has nothing to do with the yews, but comes from the word 'clypping' meaning embracing. In a ceremony probably derived from a pagan ritual the children, dressed in their party best, hold hands completely encircling the church, as a way of expressing their love and gratitude to Mother Church. With the congregation and choir they sing the hymn for the Clipping, the circle sweeping in and out towards the church like a junior Auld Lang Syne. Afterwards the children are rewarded with a Painswick bun and a 10p coin.

# Standish

If there is one churchyard that has everything, it must be Standish. It has a definite 'feel' about it, an atmosphere created by tall trees and squabbling birds among old, tilting tombs, many of them seventeenth century. Here the stonemasons have had a free hand: all the figures of classical symbolism are here: death and immortality surrounded by fruit, flowers and foliage in rich abundance.

**Plate 70.** *Carved lyre ends, Standish*

Near the early chest tomb to Samuell Beard, Yeaman, is a coffin-shaped ledger with the inscriptions along one side to Eliz Beard, 1639. This is a rare survivor; hundreds of similar ledgers will have sunk beneath the soil in the intervening 300 years.

Another unique carved chest tomb dated 1680 has two seated figures holding hands, wearing full-bottomed periwigs. They seem to be wrapped in winding sheets and each has a foot resting on a skull. The adjacent tomb has a similar single figure standing upright, also clad in a winding sheet. They are both in excellent condition, protected by trees above and by the generous overhang of the lid.

A chest tomb dated 1718 has on one side a winged figure of Father Time with scythe and hour-glass, while on the other side Death in the form of a skeleton carries a shroud over his arm and a spade, and stands on a serpent with its tail in its mouth, symbol of eternity.

The best preserved is a chest tomb to Anne wife of Samuel Niblett who died in 1676. Around them are heavy drapes of fruit and vegetables and also for some reason known only to the sculptor, prawns. The cartouche is barely legible, but beside it are two classical draped figures in headdresses with enigmatic smiles on their faces. They look like little girls; one has her head on her hand as though asleep, and each of them is resting nonchalantly on a skull.

Nearby is another tomb, evidently the work of the same sculptor because the figures have a similarity and a similar headdress. This one is holding a skull firmly by the eye socket and he has a trailing stalk of foliage over his shoulder. His friend on the other side of the cartouche is leaning on a book, apparently asleep, and both have bare chubby feet.

Another chest tomb with gadrooned corners has a rectangular end with a graphic picture of a child kneeling with hands in supplication and a book on a lectern. Above a shelf, or lid, over the child's head is the winged and bearded head of Father Time with scythe and hourglass.

There are brass plates on heavy ledgers, including one to Beate Chamberlayne who died in 1858. It reads:

Husband farewell and children dear
I am not dead but sleeping here
A virtuous wife and friend to all
Till God was pleased for me to call
Weep not for me it is in vain
I hope in Heaven to meet again.

On the other side of the church is a more recent headstone to a man who would not have been popular today:

**Plate 71.** *Chest tomb with prawns, Standish*

Rowland Smith, Gamekeeper. Forty years earth-stopper to the Berkeley Hunt. After a life of unexampled work in this parish he passed (sic) 23 Feby 1924 aged 81 years.

# Woodchester

The village of Woodchester lies dotted along the hillside between Nailsworth and Stroud. Old stone cottages cling perilously to the slope, their front doors opening straight on to narrow pavements.

To the north of the village the ruins of the old church stand among yews and chest tombs. Great oak trees line the walls and blackberries as big as marbles hang out of the hedges. Across the valley the green sward of Rodborough Common basks in the autumn sun.

The churchyard is dominated by an avenue of yew trees that meet over your head to form a dark green tunnel. At the far end is what is left of the Norman church that was demolished in 1860; all that remains is the chancel arch and the north doorway growing out of a smooth green lawn.

But it is what is under your feet that makes this churchyard one of the most precious of all time. Here it is literally true that if you scratch Gloucestershire you will find Rome, for under the smooth green sward in the centre of the churchyard lies one of our greatest Roman treasures. The existence of a Roman mosaic pavement has been known since at least since 1693, but it was not until 1789 that Samuel Lysons began the excavation, after the digging of a burial vault had revealed part of the pavement. What he found was the foundations of a great Roman villa, one of the largest and finest in England, with inner and outer courts and over sixty rooms. The pavement is fifty feet square and was the floor of the main hall, made up of over a million tesserae, each one about half an inch across. It depicts Orpheus with his lute surrounded by animals, birds and trees.

The pavement remains covered, and was last opened for public viewing nearly twenty years ago. Arthur Mee in his 'Gloucestershire' puts the time scale into perspective: 'Here in the heart of our countryside is this Roman god sitting in the earth with all the pictures encircling him. He has been here from Caesar's day to Alfred's, from Alfred's to the Conqueror's, through the days of

**Plate 72.** *Remains of Norman church, Woodchester*

**Plate 73.** *Grass lawn covering Roman pavement, Woodchester*

| Eliz | Natus | June 10th 1776 | Obiit | Dec 8th 1778 |
|------|-------|----------------|-------|--------------|
| Ann  |       | Nov 7th 1779   |       | June 27 1797 |
| John |       | July 20th 1784 |       | Nov 9th 1784 |

> Christ did by grace embrace the young
> When here upon the earth
> Such precious souls to Him belong
> He bought them at his death.

Plantaganets, Tudors and Stuarts, and still he is here, central figure of the biggest Roman mosaic still preserved in England, the hidden treasure of Woodchester with a record longer than the reigns of fifty English kings.'

A copy of the pavement has been made by the brothers Bob and Charles Woodward from photographic records, using a million and a half tesserae of stone from local quarries. At the moment it is in store; if a permanent site could be found for it, preferably in Gloucestershire, it would certainly become one of our major tourist attractions.

There is a good collection of chest tombs, including an unusual large rectangular podium carved in perpendicular style, the inscription unfortunately gone. A beautifully worked brass plate on a ledger stone is a sad reminder of the high rate of infant mortality in the eighteenth century. It reads:

This memorial is inscribed to the one son and four daughters of Nathaniel and Sarah Hillman of this parish viz.

| Eliz | Nov 20th 1774 | Apr 19th 1776 |
|------|---------------|---------------|
| Ann  | Nov 20th 1774 | Dec 9th 1778  |

By modern standards it is rather gruesome to use again the names of children that have died.

In one corner is a symbolic tomb with a plain triangle representing the Trinity on a horizontal circle, for Eternity. There is also a tomb surrounded by close railings with knobs on the corners like an old-fashioned child's cot and brambles poking out between the rails.

There is a serenity about this quiet corner of Woodchester that makes you just want to stand; to absorb the atmosphere of peace, of history underfoot, of birdsong among ancient trees in this oasis of tranquillity.

# Glossary

**Bale tomb** Chest tomb surmounted by a roll top, often incised, the ends carved into a scallop

**Bargeboards** A wooden board fixed to the overhanging gable end of a roof, often decorated.

**Beakhead** Form of decoration depicting the head of a bird or animal. Characteristic of Norman architecture.

**Body stone** Stone covering a grave which is round or oval in cross-section

**Cartouche** Carved or ornamental panel in the form of a scroll.

**Centaur** Mythological creature with head, arms and torso of a man and lower body and legs of a horse.

**Chamfer** Effect of cutting away the sharp edge where two corners of stone meet.

**Chevron** Zigzag ornamentation characteristic of Norman architecture.

**Church Ales** Festivities held in churchyards in mediaeval times to raise money.

**Classical** Style of decoration in the manner of Greek architecture

**Clerestory** Upper part of the wall of the nave and choir, containing windows.

**Coffin table** Raised block of stone under the lychgate on which the coffin was rested.

**Corbel** Block of stone, often carved, projecting from a wall and supporting roof or other structure.

**Corbel table** Connected line of corbels supporting a roof or parapet.

**Crockets** Small buds or leaves at regular intervals projecting from the sloping sides of spires or pinnacles.

**Dole table** Slab or tomb in the churchyard from which bread and alms were distributed to the poor.

**Dripstone** Projecting moulding over the heads of doorways and windows to throw off rain. Also known as hood-mould.

**Epitaph** Comment or rhyme found on tombstones to describe the character or fate of the deceased.

**Finial** A decorative top to a pinnacle, dome or gable.

**Footstone** A small stone marking the foot of the grave.

**Gadroon** Decorative moulding consisting of a series of convex flutes and curves.

**Gargoyle** Waterspout projecting from the side of the church or tower to throw rainwater clear. Often carved in the shape of animal or human heads.

**Gothic Revival** Early 19th century copy of Gothic style

**Griffin** Winged monster with the head of an eagle. Also gryphon.

**Grotesque** Caricature, usually carved in stone on exterior of church.

**Gryphon** See griffin

**Headstone** Shaped stone at the head of a grave, usually inscribed.

**Hood** Projecting upper edge of headstone

**Ledger** A flat stone covering a grave.

**Lychgate** Covered entrance to the churchyard.

**Pedestal tomb** Chest tomb that is higher than it is long. Also Podium.

**Pilaster** Rectangular column projecting from a wall.

**Podium** See Pedestal

**Quatrefoil** Four-leafed ornamental infilling to a circle

**Standing stone** Prehistoric stone erected on pagan sites

**String course** A moulding or projecting course of stonework running horizontally along a wall.

**Trefoil** Three-leafed ornamental infilling to a circle.

**Tympanum** Space between the lintel of a doorway and the arch above. often carved.

**Weepers** Mourning figures often seen on decorated chest tombs.

**Wyvern** Heraldic winged beast with a serpent's tail and dragon's head.

# Bibliography

**Bailey Brian.** *Churchyards of England and Wales.* Robert Hale 1987

**Bigland Ralph.** *Historical Monuments and Genealogical Collections.* Bristol & Gloucestershire Archaeological Society (no date)

**Blackler Beaver H.**(Ed) *Gloucestershire Notes & Queries.* W Kent & Co 1881

**Brill Edith.** *Cotswold Ways.* Robert Hale 1985

**Burman and Stapleton.** *The Churchyards Handbook.* Church House Publishing 1988

**Burgess Frederick.** *English Churchyard Memorials.* Lutterworth Press 1963

**Child Mark.** *Discovering Churchyards.* Shire Publications 1989

**Clifton-Taylor Alec.** *English Parishes Churches* Oxford University Press 1989

**Darvill Timothy.** *Prehistoric Gloucestershire.* Alan Sutton 1987

**Greenoak Francesca.** *God's Acre.* Orbis 1985

**Hill Susan.** *Spirit of the Cotswolds.* Michael Joseph 1988

**Hudson Kenneth.** *Churchyards and Cemeteries.* Bodley Head 1984

**Laundon Jack R.** *Lichens* Shire Books 1986

**Lindley Kenneth.** *Of Graves and Epitaphs.* Hutchinson 1965

**Mee Arthur.** *Gloucestershire.* Hodder and Stoughton 1947

**Moriarty Denis.** *Buildings of the Cotswolds* Victor Gollancz 1989

**Verey David.** *Cotswold Churches* Alan Sutton 1982

**Wright Geoffrey N.** *Discovering Epitaphs.* Shire Publications Ltd 1987

# Useful Addresses

**Church and Conservation Project**, The Arthur Rank Centre, National Agricultural Centre, Stoneleigh, Warwickshire. CV8 2LZ Tel: 0203 696969

**English Nature** (for the Yew Tree Campaign) 1 Kensington Gore, London SW7 2AR Tel: 071 823 8842

**English Heritage**, Fortress House, 23 Savile Row, London W1X 1AB Tel: 071 973 3000

**Gloucestershire Wildlife Trust**, Dulverton Building, Robinswood Hill Country Park, Reservoir Road, Gloucester. Tel: 0452 383333

**Gloucester Diocesan Committee**, Church House, College Green, Gloucester GL1 2LY. Tel: 0452 410022

**Memorials by Artists**. Snape Priory, Saxmundham, Suffolk IP17 1SA Tel: 072 888 8934

# Index

*Italics indicates illustrations*